KNOW
BEFORE
YOU GO

PREPARING FOR A GREAT MISSION

KNOW BEFORE YOU GO

PREPARING FOR A GREAT MISSION

CHRIS DEAVER

Covenant Communications, Inc.

Covenant

Cover image *A Road Less Traveled* © Jeffrey H. Craven

Cover design copyrighted 2004 by Covenant Communications, Inc.

Published by Covenant Communications, Inc.
American Fork, Utah

Printed in Canada
First Printing: March 2004

08 07 06 05 04   10 9 8 7 6 5 4 3 2 1

ISBN 1-59156-443-3

Advance Praise for *Know Before You Go*

"*Know Before You Go* is a unique, creative approach to making a missionary's experience more lasting and meaningful. The content is well done and well thought out. Both upcoming missionaries and their parents would benefit from this resource as they plan to make their next two years memorable and successful."

—LaVell Edwards, retired head football coach,
Brigham Young University

"Upon reading Christopher Deaver's *Know Before You Go*, I couldn't help but wonder, What if I had had the valuable lessons contained in his book prior to my mission? I think I could have been more effective. It's an interesting thought. You read it. See what you think. The really great missionaries carry with them a loving spirit, but teaching, like acting, requires skill, research, and diligent study. Thanks, Chris, for a terrific manual!"

—Don Bluth, Director of An American Tail *and* Anastasia

"Good book, well written. A positive portrayal that many young missionaries can identify with and benefit from."

—Randy Bott, former mission president, BYU professor

"An excellent read not just for those young men and women preparing for a full-time mission, but for anyone serious about better preparing themselves for the mission of life."

—Hyrum Smith, inventor of the Franklin Planner™, and
author of Where Eagles Rest

ACKNOWLEDGEMENTS

To my mother and father, Devi and Tom, who never stop encouraging me to dream. To my grandmother, Violet Deaver, whose faith—like the mothers of the stripling warriors—has blessed generations. To Marianne for her faith, Ed for his mission stories, Rebekah (whose name I am *now* spelling correctly) for her courage, Andrew for his delectable suggestions, Matt for his friendship, and Melissa for being Melissa. To my mission presidents Theron D. Rose and Stephen L. Jensen for their love and unforgettable counsel that blessed my life in a dramatic way. To my "other families" of Peru—the Camposes, Diazes, Guerras, and Paredeses—for sharing so many adventures in teaching. To my mentor, Randy Bott, for his unwavering commitment to the doctrines of the gospel of Jesus Christ and feedback that seriously affected the development of this book. To my friend Joseph Lewis for his boldness, Elder Tyson Allen for his charity, Luke Drake for his editing, Angela Colvin and Peter Jasinski for the writing help, Dave Howell for the MTC pep talks, Ken Shelton for his mission insights, John Bytheway for his suggestions, Richard Herold for his contagious love for teaching, and Stephen Covey for his motivating words.

TABLE OF CONTENTS

INTRODUCTION

Are you ready to serve with all your heart, might, mind, and strength, nonstop and full-time in a place you've never been, with people you've never met before? It's time to get ready for the greatest adventure of all time! *Know Before You Go* will help you get into the powerful, spirit-driven missionary mind-set. Here you'll find specific, principled suggestions to guide you.

This book is for anyone with an appetite for mission success but especially for future missionaries interested in serving the Lord in a faithful way.

When I was younger, I thought books were a waste of time, and cartoons were insightful creations that would mold my character. Growing up, I haven't really changed my mind about cartoons, but I have about *books*. This book will help you see a mission for what it is. A commandment? Yes, for young men, but more than that. A duty? Yep, but still more than that. It's an ADVENTURE!

You will find excitement, challenge, fun, and adventure in the difficult circumstances you face when you have the Spirit. You will be amazed at the adventures you start to have, because everything becomes more fun. Classes you once slept through become explorations of beautiful new insights; church talks that seemed like tedious forms of torture become sermons that catch your spirit on fire; and formerly boring chores become opportunities for serious spiritual growth.

You are embarking on a journey that will be like creating a movie masterpiece. Which movies have uplifted you? Quality movies are those that inspire excellence through a central character whose life and mission are exemplary. Inspiring movies are created long before they hit the big screen—written in every detail, then directed and produced for a large audience (they don't magically appear on screen).

Have you ever made a home video with your family? It can be a lot of fun (especially if you can catch your grandpa snoring). True film-making, however, is both lots of fun *and* work. First, a writer sits down at his desk and starts to brainstorm. His ideas slowly form into a vision of the big picture. The writer wants to create the best story he can, one that will capture, entertain, and uplift the audience. Once he has a script he feels comfortable with, he hands it off to the director for filming.

When the director receives the script, he plans how to execute every camera shot. Then, he starts filming, recording specific events as actors and actresses play them out using lines from the script. Frequently, the director calls for "action" to get things rolling.

Throughout this entire process, the producer oversees the making of the movie. His job is to make sure every little detail is taken care of, and that the writer and director are having their needs met with respect to making a great film. The producer offers resources to help in the process.

As you go through your own process of creating a powerful mission story, think like a writer and director. Catch the vision of what kind of missionary you want to be and write it down in the spaces provided in this book. Follow the instructions provided and watch how you change. Notice how you become a greater servant in the Lord's (the real producer's) hands.

In this book, you will find three headings at the end of each chapter to help you set and achieve righteous objectives. Here is an overview of how each suggestion will help you:

PRODUCER'S POWER TIP: Along the way, you will be given producer power tips from inspired servants of the Lord to help you stay focused in the process of creating a powerful mission story.

WRITER'S CORNER: Here you can write down the ideas that come to you. Think "outside the box," and jot down thoughts no matter how crazy they seem at the time. You will also have a chance to write down your vision of the service you want to perform.

DIRECTOR'S ACTION: Get deeper into the "action" of changing your life with Jesus Christ by following the ideas under this heading.

This is not an all-inclusive, flawless book with *all* the answers to the "whats," "hows," and "whys" of missionary service. It *is* a presentation of principles that have helped missionaries, including Ammon, Nephi, and Alma, to serve powerfully. Now, let's talk about the most important thing: what you need to Know Before You Go!

PRODUCER'S POWER TIP
President Spencer W. Kimball stated, "There is a spiritual adventure in doing missionary work." (*Ensign*, Oct. 1977, 7)

WRITER'S CORNER:
How can you plan for your mission adventure?

_____

_____

_____

_____

_____

_____

_____

_____

_____

What kind of mission stories do you want to have?

_____

_____

_____

_____

_____

_____

_____

_____

_____

DIRECTOR'S ACTION
Start thinking and seriously praying daily about the impact you want to have on others through your service to the Lord. Think and read about great missionaries like Ammon, Abinadi, Alma, and Joseph Smith and their mission adventures. Read Alma chapters 5 and 18, Mosiah 13, and Joseph Smith—History.

CHAPTER ONE

The Atonement: Your Personal Power Source

The Atonement is your personal power source. What you say as you teach people the gospel must direct their minds and hearts to Gethsemane, Calvary, and the garden tomb so they can feel what the Savior did for them. A focus on the Atonement will make your actions powerful and breathe eternal life into situations on your mission. It will give you the confidence you need to knock doors, teach, and baptize. Jeffrey R. Holland, in an article titled "Missionary Work and the Atonement," emphasized:

> The Prophet Joseph Smith once declared that all things "which pertain to our religion are only appendages" to the Atonement of Jesus Christ. In like manner and for the same reasons, every truth that a missionary or member teaches is only an appendage to the central message of all time—that Jesus is the Christ . . . the Savior and Redeemer of the world. . . .
>
> Our basic message is that with a complete offering of His body, His blood, and the anguish of His spirit, Christ atoned for the initial transgression of Adam and Eve in the Garden of Eden, and also for the personal sins of everyone else who would ever live in this world from Adam to the end of time.
>
> Some of those blessings are unconditional, such as the gift of the Resurrection. Other of the blessings . . . are very conditional, requiring the keeping of commandments, the performance of ordinances, and living the life of a disciple of Christ.

> Either way, the essential message of the gospel . . . is this from the Master's own lips: "I am the way, the truth, and the life: no man cometh unto the Father, but by me." Thus the Atonement of Christ, which makes that return to the Father possible, is rightfully seen as the central fact, the crucial foundation, and the chief doctrine of the great and eternal plan of salvation, . . . which we are called to teach. (*Ensign*, Mar. 2001, 8)

Learn about the Atonement before your mission. As a missionary, the Atonement is what makes you want to get up in the morning; it motivates you to share truth and love others. To be a powerful missionary, get to know Jesus Christ and what He has done and is doing for you (see D&C 19:16–19).

Before my mission, I had heard hundreds of testimonies about the suffering and love of Jesus Christ, but I didn't understand how others could feel that way. Don't get me wrong; I never doubted the divinity of Jesus Christ, but I only understood the Atonement as an idea, and not in terms of how it affected *me*.

One night I prayed and thanked Heavenly Father for the Atonement of His Son and sincerely asked to understand it on a more personal level. As I listened for an answer, I experienced a peaceful feeling in my heart. I realized that Jesus Christ not only suffered for me but could feel and understand *my* challenges, weaknesses, and pains, and that He was right there, cheering me on. That answer to my prayer transformed me. I could now testify to investigators that I knew Jesus Christ could save them, give them hope, and help them feel pure love.

Experience the Atonement *now.* As you partake of the sacrament each week, think specifically about the Savior and His sacrifice for you. Envision what He did and how He feels about you. Magnify your calling, teach friends the gospel, and read the Book of Mormon. Serious study of the Book of Mormon will open your eyes to the Savior's atoning power in your life. As you pray intensely in gratitude for the Atonement, you will come to know Jesus Christ.

PRODUCER'S POWER TIP

Howard W. Hunter, in an article titled "Standing as Witnesses of God," wrote:

> If we can pattern our life after the Master, and take his teaching and example as the supreme pattern for our own, we will not find it difficult to be consistent and loyal in every walk of life, for we will be committed to a single, sacred standard of conduct and belief. (*Ensign*, May 1990, 60)

WRITER'S CORNER

Write your feelings about Jesus Christ and how you feel about what He willingly did for you.

_____

_____

_____

_____

_____

_____

_____

_____

_____

_____

_____

_____

_____

_____

_____

DIRECTOR'S ACTION

Understand the Atonement better by fasting and praying for someone who needs help in his or her life (a family member or friend). Search selected chapters in the Book of Mormon that teach about the Atonement: 2 Nephi 9, Mosiah 4, Alma 7, or Alma 36.

CHAPTER TWO

Create a Powerful Mission Story

Your decisions will affect your eternal destiny. Think of some important decisions from the past: What if Nephi decided he would neither "go" nor "do"? What if Joseph of Egypt, when tempted by Potiphar's wife, decided that "lying" down a few minutes on the couch in the dark would be okay? What if Joseph Smith, instead of getting up that special spring morning, decided to roll over and sleep some more? One decision *does* matter and it *can* make the eternal difference.

I don't remember a specific day when I suddenly announced, "I'm going to serve a mission"—I think I always wanted to. I do remember when my dad asked me how serious I was about serving a full-time mission. I thought, "Is this man I have lived with for over seventeen years *insane*? Of course I'm serious. But, wait a minute! He's asking *me* about how serious *I* am about a mission. Why doesn't he just tell me I *have* to go?"

My father wanted me to decide. Though he could talk forever about why I should serve a mission, he could not decide for me if I would serve. "If ye have desires to serve, ye are called to the work" (D&C 4:3).

A friend of mine once emphasized with feeling to me, "The Lord is hard-pressed for leaders!" He is, and He needs you. He needs your knuckles to knock doors and your voice to declare His everlasting gospel with pure boldness. He does not do it alone, and neither Nephi, Alma, Moroni, Mormon, nor Joseph Smith will replace you. It's time to decide.

One missionary suggests: "Decide NOW! Decide that no matter what happens, you are going on a mission and you're going to stay on your mission. . . . Don't wait until you're set apart! Live the life of a disciple NOW!"

Once you have decided to be a powerful missionary, you may start to notice opposition. Peers, friends, even family members may question your decision. You must be determined you will serve the Lord honorably at all costs. Don't let the weaknesses of others (or even yourself) keep you from doing what the Lord absolutely *needs* you to do. Yoda (that's right, the old, two-foot-nothing alien from *Star Wars*) once said: "Do or do not. There is no try." Mission preparation is doing. *To do* requires serious determination. And one powerful way to get that determination is envisioning your success as a missionary.

Envision Your Mission Story

Imagine this: Your friends and family have been telling you about an interesting new film and you have become excited to finally see it. You enter the theater on opening night with your family. You grab popcorn and a soda and find an open seat.

As you sit down with your family, you notice all your friends are there too! To your left are your bishop and stake president. To your right, you notice people you have met during the course of your life. "This *must* be a good movie," you think to yourself.

The lights dim, the film rolls, and your name appears in bright red letters across the screen with: *THIS IS YOUR MISSION*. It includes everything you ever said and thought (in subtitles!) from start to finish. At this point, you start to sink a little in your chair.

Though it may sound a little scary, your mission is so important that you will want to act as if all were watching it. Your children will one day ask about your mission story and may even open their eyes wide and "ooh" and "ahh" when you tell details of what you were able to do with the help of the Lord. Your grand key to success is to come unto Christ. He will help you prepare for and carry out a powerful mission.

> Yea, come unto Christ, and be perfected in him, and deny yourselves of all ungodliness, and love God with all your might, mind

and strength, then is his grace sufficient for you, that by his grace ye may be perfect in Christ; and if by the grace of God ye are perfect in Christ, ye can in nowise deny the power of God. (Moro. 10:32)

You are both the writer and director of your mission story. In many ways you can determine how interesting and inspiring your movie will be.

Create your own adventure! You choose what you want your mission story to look like, be like, and feel like. No one can force you to create a great mission story, but wouldn't it be great to do something your parents, friends, converts, and especially the Lord would be proud of? You determine the ultimate outcome in your mission.

Think about your mission story as an adventure. What makes an adventure GREAT? To get a clear picture of this, compare the book of Nephi to the fictitious "Book of Laman." For the record, there is no Book of Laman; but if there were one, what would it say? "I, Laman, having been born of stupid parents, therefore I was taught everything boring of my father; and having seen many afflictions from my idiot brother, Nephi, I was forced to do stupid, boring things all my days." Obviously, this does not sound like something uplifting, or even true. What about "Laman the Movie"? It would include hours of complaining, murmuring, and disobeying God's commandments.

The best mission stories, like the best movies, show strong characters who progress and create an interesting adventure. Think of the film *The Other Side of Heaven*, the movie based on the mission experiences of Elder John H. Groberg. It includes powerful experiences from his mission—learning the language, teaching the people, and overcoming a dangerous storm through faith. It is based directly on what Elder Groberg did on his mission.

Think of the mission stories of Ammon, Alma, and the other greats in the scriptures. Remember Ammon? He was converted, went to the Lamanites to teach them the gospel, was brought before King Lamoni, and offered to serve the king for the rest of his days. He "disarmed" those who attacked the king's sheep, and then taught the gospel to King Lamoni. Talk about a mission story!

Alma the Younger, after his conversion, went from city to city teaching the gospel, bringing people the word that "had more powerful effect upon the minds of the people than the sword or anything else" (Alma 31:5).

Paul the Apostle diligently taught the message of Jesus Christ in the face of danger, but he bore his testimony without fear of any man. Near the end of his life he could say, "I have fought a good fight, I have finished my course, I have kept the faith" (2 Tim. 4:8).

Don't try to create a great mission from nothing. Explore the best stories ever created on the big screen of life. You are surrounded by awesome missions in the scriptures, the lives of those you admire, and the perfect life of Jesus Christ. The Savior lived the greatest mission story of all-time—the one to be imitated above all others.

Understanding You and Your Mission

Create a powerful mission story by building upon the foundation of who you are. And, who exactly are *you*? What is *your* role in the eternal plan? Consider these words of Ezra Taft Benson:

> For nearly six thousand years, God has held *you* in reserve to make your appearance in the final days before the Second Coming of the Lord. . . . While our generation will be comparable in wickedness to the days of Noah, when the Lord cleansed the earth by flood, there is a major difference this time. It is that God has saved for the final inning some of His strongest children, who will help bear off the Kingdom triumphantly. That is where you come in, for you are the generation that must be prepared to meet your God. . . .
>
> In all ages prophets have looked down through the corridors of time to our day. Billions of the deceased and those yet to be born have their eyes on us. Make no mistake about it—you are a marked generation. There has never been more expected of the faithful in such a short period of time than there is of us. Never before on the face of this earth have the forces of evil and the forces of good been as well organized. Now is the great day of the

devil's power. But now is also the great day of the Lord's power, with the greatest number ever of priesthood holders on the earth. (*Teachings of Ezra Taft Benson* [1988], 104–105; italics added)

As a missionary, you are called of God to do what you have desired to do for over six thousand years. Joseph Smith declared, "*Every* man [or woman] who has a calling to minister to the inhabitants of the world was ordained to *that very purpose* in the Grand Council of heaven before this world was" (*Teachings of the Prophet Joseph Smith*, sel. Joseph Fielding Smith [1976], 365; italics added).

The work of the Lord is not casual! It is not to be taken for granted! Every little thing you do in the service of the Lord creates waves that move lives toward or away from God. It may not seem like you are saving the universe or even the world (after all, you can't hear any "danger theme song" music playing in the background of your life), but you are saving people—one soul at a time. Each soul represents millions of righteous people. Each soul is a potential *god-in-the-making*. You can count the seeds in an apple, but you can't count the apples in a seed.

President Kimball described the value of your work this way:

> You are in the greatest work in the world, and nothing in this world can compare to it. Building homes and bridges is nothing. Building worlds is nothing compared to the lives you are building. The saving of mortal lives isn't any important accomplishment as compared to what you are doing. You might go out here to one of these cemeteries and raise the dead, even a thousand or ten thousand of them, and you haven't done anything compared to what you are doing when you are saving people. (*Teachings of Spencer W. Kimball* [1982], 547)

Unlock the door to a powerful mission by seeking the help of the Lord. Join Him in His mission. What is *His* mission? "This is my work and my glory—to bring to pass the immortality and eternal life of man" (Moses 1:39).

With the Lord's help you can start writing your mission story now! You may be thinking, "Is this Deaver guy *crazy*? He hasn't even told me where to start or what to do . . . I'm not even *on* my mission yet!" That's exactly the point! Once you're physically on your mission, preparation time will be over—it will be time to just do it.

PRODUCER'S POWER TIP

Doctrine and Covenants 46:7 states: "But ye are commanded in all things to ask of God, who giveth liberally; and that which the spirit testifies unto you even so I would that ye should do in all holiness of heart, walking uprightly before me, considering the end of your salvation."

WRITER'S CORNER

Imagine yourself watching your entire mission experience or "movie" through the eyes of four particular people: the Lord, your future spouse, one of your future children, and someone to whom you taught the gospel.

How do you want the Lord to feel about your mission story once He has watched it all?

That I have been a faithful Servant on earth

How do you want your future spouse to feel about it?

I did marry the man of my dreams

How do you want your future child to feel about it?

I want to be like him Someday

How do you want someone to whom you taught the gospel to feel about it?

I   am   Sure   lucky

he   taught   me

DIRECTOR'S ACTION

Do whatever it takes to make your mission story everything you and the Lord want it to be. Return occasionally to what you wrote, review it, and adjust your direction as you feel necessary. You may later find you left out something important. If so, go back and write it in (or draw it in).

CHAPTER THREE

Plan to Make It Happen!

Once you've got the vision for your mission story, you need a plan to achieve powerful results. To plan effectively, focus on the Seven P's of Planning:

1. Purpose
2. Principles
3. Priorities
4. Personas
5. Plans
6. Performances
7. Patterns

Purpose. Effective planning begins with a clear purpose. Purpose is the reason for the mission to be accomplished. For Jesus Christ (and for you, as a missionary) it is to "bring to pass the immortality and eternal life of man" (Moses 1:39).

Principles. Once you have established your purpose, that great big "why" behind what you do, move forward by deciding what principles will help you achieve it—or the big "how." Principles are eternal truths that create long-term results, such as "Love one another." These truths don't ever disappear or diminish in power. Principles, when applied correctly, will lead you to consistent successes.

Priorities. Let your principles determine your priorities. Priorities are specific areas to which you give time, whether you realize it or not. One priority would be that of loving your family, based on the principle of loving one another.

When you set priorities, you need to determine what activities will help you spend time making progress according to your purpose and principles. You might ask yourself questions like "How does television watching time rate compared to time spent doing service?" or "Should I focus more on serving my family or earning money?" Use the following questions as a basic gauge to prioritize your activities: Is it helping to build me physically, spiritually, emotionally, mentally, or otherwise? Is it helping to build someone else in any of these ways? If not, think twice about that activity—because it's probably not important.

Personas. Once you have set your course, based on godly principles and priorities, your work is only partly finished. Now, you must recognize your personas, or roles, which the Lord expects you to fulfill. Jesus Christ worked daily within different roles during His mission on earth. He was *Savior*, the one who would literally save you and me from sin and death; *Judge*, or He who would set forth righteous judgment; *Example*, He who lived a perfect life for us to follow.

The Savior was also the *Son of God, son of earthly parents, brother, carpenter, friend, healer,* and *leader of the Church.* Jesus Christ was not imbalanced in His approach in fulfilling these roles. In fact, He was perfectly balanced in every endeavor. This meant that sometimes he had to express softer or tougher love, depending on the situation, or teach essential doctrine, or heal someone. In other words, His life patterns flowed from His understanding of His particular roles. This takes not only great desire, but powerful confidence. Know, like Jesus Christ knew, that Heavenly Father will back you up when you work for Him.

Plans. Plans ought to be set based upon your principles, priorities, and personas. As you know, plans are specific instructions for achieving a goal. Write down goals that are Specific, Measurable, Attainable, Realistic, and Time-Based (SMART). Once you've listed your goals, break them down into smaller steps, then attack them with everything you've got.

Performances. You will achieve high performance as you work hard at your principle- and purpose-based plans. As you do, your best performances will become powerful, unchanging patterns.

Patterns. Patterns, in the godliest sense of the word, are those habits you have established in your life that lead to solid, positive results.

Daily scripture study and prayer are perfect examples. Additionally, a weekly service project is a rewarding pattern. Set Christlike patterns in your life, and they will become part of your permanent character. Powerful missionaries develop immovable, godly habits.

Measuring Success

Measure your performance as you move through this process of establishing your personal principles, priorities, personas, patterns, and plans. Be aware of the positive results you achieve and the areas you can improve.

Focus positively on your goals. One successful sister missionary suggests: "Write down your goals before you begin preparing. What you want to accomplish, how you will accomplish it, the amount of time you have to accomplish it, etc. Keep your goals where you can look at them often. Check your progress." Envision successes before they happen. Look at your goals every day. Draw pictures or get photos of your goals as realities, hang them up, and look at them daily. Write objectives in your journal, or write them on sticky pads and put them up everywhere to remember. Elder M. Russell Ballard said:

> I believe you can train yourself to become a positive thinker, but you must cultivate a desire to develop the skill of setting personal worthy and realistic goals. . . . I am so thoroughly convinced that if we don't set goals in our life and learn how to master the technique of living to reach our goals, we can reach a ripe old age and look back on our life only to see that we reached but a small part of our full potential. When one learns to master the principle of setting a goal, he will then be able to make a great difference in the results he attains in this life. . . .
>
> I would suggest that if you want to have success in the goal-setting process, you learn to write your goals down. I would even put them in a very prominent place—on your mirror or on the refrigerator door. Keep your goals in front of you, in writing. Then, with the desire to reach your written goals, you will be more willing to pay the price that successful goal-oriented people must pay. (*Ensign*, June 1983, 69–70)

One exercise that helps to measure and increase performance is to keep a "Power Journal" wherein you record all the great things you are accomplishing with the help of the Lord. This helps you build confidence and power to continue the achievement cycle.

Another way of building confidence is to spend thirty seconds at night, before you retire, talking to yourself in the mirror. I know, it sounds crazy, but it's not. Look in the mirror, smile, and tell yourself how you appreciate all the great things you are achieving right now. List specific accomplishments to yourself that you achieved that day, and you will feel empowered to do even better tomorrow. Believe me, this works. Success breeds success.

Measure your daily performance against your goal, and see if you do it. In setting goals, be specific and write down measurable and attainable goals, then break each goal down into bite-size, weekly goals. Don't set vague goals like "Have charity"—there's no when or how. A better goal is "Pray sincerely for charity two times each day."

As you record a goal consider these basic questions:

1. **What:** What is my goal? Is it *specific, measurable,* and *attainable*? (e.g., I will study for one hour a day to learn Spanish.)

2. **Why:** Why do I want to achieve this goal? What is my motivation? Is it Christlike?

3. **Where:** In what place or frame of reference do I need to achieve this goal? Is it with the investigators in my area? Is it in my personal life?

4. **When:** By when will I achieve this goal? Am I remembering that goals are a means to an end, and not the end itself?

5. **Who:** Which people (companion, mission president, the Lord) will be part of or involved in my goal? Who will I rely upon to help me to complete my goal?

6. **How:** What course of action will I take in order to achieve this goal? What will I commit to do? What am I willing to sacrifice to

get what I want? What will I hope, based upon my obedience, that the Lord may do for me (see D&C 82:10)?

7. **Hint:** What goal would naturally come next? How does the fulfillment of this first goal lead to the fulfillment of the next?

As the author of your own mission story, always rethink your attitude and actions and seek the help of the Lord to adjust them to His will. Set apart an hour each week (preferably on Sunday) for a "personal inventory." In that hour, ponder and focus on what is most important to you; review your mission story, goals, and your performance from the past week. Afterwards, plan and pray about your next week. Also, set apart ten to fifteen minutes every day to briefly review your plans for the next day. You can even draw (with stick men) what you are going to do the next day. This will help you visualize your performance before it actually happens and prepare you mentally for success.

Some valuable planning pages are included at the end of this chapter so you can copy and use them to plan for your mission monthly, weekly, and daily. Use these or some type of planner to guide your efforts. Either way, start planning today.

Becoming the Best You

Some future missionaries believe the Missionary Training Center (MTC) has a magical door you walk through to automatically become a powerful gospel teacher. Though the mantle of a missionary will give you greater capacity to teach, reaching your potential takes daily preparation. What would happen if a basketball player told his coach, "Coach, I don't need practice—just put me in for the big games?" When that player walks onto the court, he will not play anywhere near his potential.

Be bolder than you've ever been. Half measures only count half. Put your "whole might, mind, and soul" into your life's work and you will get "whole" results. Set more specific goals now, within your roles. If you want the Lord to feel that you gave 100 percent in home teaching or visiting teaching, then give 100 percent at it. This will add up and build continued successes. The mothers of the stripling warriors focused on being great moms, and that caused a chain reaction that saved the Nephite nation, and created a powerful mission story that is still enthusiastically told today.

Focus on becoming. Don't live in the past; emphasize the future and how the Lord sees you (your potential), then determine *how* to get there. Don't ignore completely where you are at—that would not be wise. Be honest with yourself. Honesty, however, is not "I am the stupidest person alive" or "I'll never get it." If you once had a terrible, embarrassing moment that haunts you to this day, forget about it! Don't let your past tell your future what to do.

The Lord knows you and wants to work with you in accomplishing meaningful goals. You can achieve righteous desires in anything from developing a gift from God to purifying your heart through repentance. You can always do more; achieve more; aspire for more greatness; inspire others more. But first, you have to *want* it.

You are given according to your desires. Alma stated, "I know that he granteth unto men according to their desire, whether it be unto death or unto life" (Alma 29:4). If you really want to witness enduring conversion in your investigators and less-actives, you will see it. Ammon was motivated by charity to serve King Lamoni with all his heart, then he saw the fruits of his desires in the conversion of thousands of Heavenly Father's children.

In your quest to perfect yourself, don't set goals to change other people. Instead, set a goal to influence others to come unto Christ through your work in prayers, persuasion, and persistence. The Lord never forces people into conversion, but He will help others feel the Spirit through you. Avoid creating goals, especially baptismal goals, which are based solely upon the agency of another person. Focus, instead, on what you must do to help the people feel the Spirit and then choose for themselves.

Keep your goals set on the "ideal you" and your mind will adapt to seeing that wonderful, powerful, testimony-charged you. Pretty soon, you will start surprising yourself as you become that Christlike person you aspire to be.

Execute

My mission means *everything* to me, but it has only come to mean so much through the earnest effort I put into it. I remember when my companion and I arrived in a brand-new area, and we had no one to teach. We sat down and created a series of goals to stretch us and achieve the positive results we felt the Lord wanted at that time. We wanted to include the members more in our teaching. We had noticed that people in the ward had grown somewhat frigid in their missionary efforts and needed a boost. We committed to one another and the Lord that we would only teach the second to sixth discussions if a member was present.

To be honest, I was concerned with the boldness of the goal. What would we do if the members didn't want to support the work? How many discussions could we give? Those concerns quickly faded as we faithfully went about our work and invited and encouraged members to accompany us and share faithful testimony at our discussions. I cannot begin to describe the miraculous change that came about in that ward because of the execution of that one goal. Hearts were lifted, returned missionaries who had set aside the work became our greatest allies and referral-givers, and families were brought into the Church.

Some people feel they can't do anything to prepare for great events like missions. They think they have to physically be there first. That is, quite frankly, a big, fat lie. You can do an astounding amount of preparation beforehand. Set Super-Missionary habits in place right now. Direct your life! Take control and make it happen. Make the best mission story through careful planning, then work, work, work, and more work (that's a lot of "work," but that's what it takes).

PRODUCER'S POWER TIP
Doctrine and Covenants 58:26–28 gives the following counsel:

> For behold, it is not meet that I should command in all things;
> for he that is compelled in all things, the same is a slothful and
> not a wise servant; wherefore he receiveth no reward
>
> Verily I say, men should be anxiously engaged in a good cause,
> and do many things of their own free will, and bring to pass
> much righteousness;
>
> For the power is in them, wherein they are agents unto them-
> selves. And inasmuch as men do good they shall in nowise lose
> their reward.

WRITER'S CORNER
What are the most important principles you want to live your
mission and life by? (e.g., love, lightheartedness, etc.)

charity
respect
love

What are your highest priorities? (e.g., magnify calling, etc.)
bringing people to Christ

What are your personas, or roles, right now? (e.g., teacher, student, etc.)

1. _Student_
2. _____
3. _____
4. _____
5. _____
6. _____
7. _____

What patterns, or habits, do you want to establish in each role? (e.g., As a preparing missionary, I want to pray three times a day.)

1. _pray_
2. _study scriptures_
3. _____
4. _____
5. _____
6. _____
7. _____

DIRECTOR'S ACTION
Write down a power plan to achieve a righteous desire you have.

What: _____
_____

Why: _____
_____

Where: _____
_____

When: _____
_____

Who: _____
_____

How: _____
_____

Hint: _____
_____

Come back to this page in a week, then a month, then a year from now and see how you are performing in these areas.

Here are a few planning pages. One is your Mission Story, where you can write the principles, priorities, personas, patterns, plans, and performances you expect from yourself during those special one-and-a-half or two years. You can photocopy the other two sheets, which are a weekly planner to plan and achieve weekly goals (or buy a planner or create your own).

My Mission Story

_____

_____

_____

_____

_____

_____

_____

_____

_____

_____

_____

_____

_____

_____

_____

_____

_____

_____

_____

_____

_____

_____

_____

_____

MY POWER PLAN FOR THE WEEK OF _____

	SUN	MON	TUES	WED	THURS	FRI	SAT
7 A.M.							
8 A.M.							
9 A.M.							
10 A.M.							
11 A.M.							
12 P.M.							
1 P.M.							
2 P.M.							
3 P.M.							
4 P.M.							
5 P.M.							
6 P.M.							
7 P.M.							
8 P.M.							
9 P.M.							
10 P.M.							

Goals to achieve this week:

	Planned	Reviewed	Achieved
1.	☐	☐	☐
2.	☐	☐	☐
3.	☐	☐	☐
4.	☐	☐	☐
5.	☐	☐	☐
6.	☐	☐	☐
7.	☐	☐	☐
8.	☐	☐	☐
9.	☐	☐	☐
10.	☐	☐	☐

CHAPTER FOUR

Powerful Spiritual Preparation

Some prospective missionaries don't see the reasons behind careful mission preparation. They might say, "I can do what I want now, and repent later . . . the most important thing is that I *go* on a mission." Satan loves for missionaries to believe that. Procrastinating may work in some easy high school classes, but it *cannot* work in missionary preparation (see Alma 12:24). Elder M. Russell Ballard stated:

> The day of the "repent and go" missionary is over. You know what I'm talking about, don't you, my young brothers? Some young men have the mistaken idea that they can be involved in sinful behavior and then repent when they're eighteen and a half so they can go on their mission at nineteen. While it is true that you can repent of sins, you may or you may not qualify to serve. (*Ensign*, Nov. 2002, 48)

Powerful spiritual preparation is essential to missionary service. Begin spiritually preparing for your mission now by focusing on converting yourself. You cannot convert beyond your own conversion. There is no such thing as lifting someone to a higher plane if you are not already on a higher plane. The rigorous path of conversion, which you will be expected to help your investigators through, will have to be trodden by you beforehand. When you teach them faith, you will need to have exercised faith in your life already. When you talk about repentance, you will need to have experienced beforehand the cleansing power of the Atonement in your own life. Live the gospel now so you can receive the blessings Ammon talked about.

Yea, he that *repenteth* and *exerciseth faith*, and *bringeth forth good works*, and *prayeth continually without ceasing*—unto such it is given to know the mysteries of God; yea, unto such it shall be given to *reveal things which never have been revealed*; yea, and it shall be given unto such *to bring thousands of souls to repentance*, even as it has been given unto us to bring these our brethren to repentance. (Alma 26:22; italics added)

Powerful preparation requires understanding the principle that you are in control of you. What happens if the writer of a movie doesn't do anything? Absolutely, positively, 100 percent nothing. You are responsible, and you control the direction of your life story according to the will of the Lord. It was once said, "God cast a vote for man, Satan cast one against, and yours is the deciding vote." How will *you* vote?

Your decision now to prepare spiritually for your mission will make all the difference. As you work on your own conversion, commit to total obedience and building a Christlike character.

Total Obedience

President Ezra Taft Benson wrote:

Prepare yourselves spiritually. A spiritual person obeys *all* the Lord's commandments. He prays to our Heavenly Father, and he gives service to others.

. . . You're learning now to keep the commandments of the Lord. As you do so, you will have His Spirit to be with you. You'll feel good about yourselves. You can't *do* wrong and *feel* right. It's impossible! One of the great lessons that I learned on my first mission was the principle of *total obedience*. (*Ensign*, May 1985, 45)

What is *total obedience*? Total obedience is what the two thousand stripling warriors did—obey every rule and commandment with faith in the Lord. Total obedience is not going through the Missionary Handbook, or the *For the Strength of Youth* pamphlet and selecting (like a menu) which rules one will or won't obey—after all, selective obedience is disobedience. Total obedience is not looking for ways to hide oneself from others, or to "not get caught." In life, everything you do, say, and even think is recorded. Total obedience is not falling for Satan's lies, like "Everybody's doing it" or "That mission rule doesn't apply to me or this mission" or "I can always repent later."

Total obedience is not blind obedience. Elder Boyd K. Packer emphasized why we are obedient:

> Those who talk of blind obedience may appear to know many things, but they do not understand the doctrines of the gospel. There is an obedience that comes from a knowledge of the truth that transcends any external form of control. We are not obedient because we are blind, we are obedient because we can see. (*Ensign*, May 1983, 66)

The Lord declared, "I, the Lord, am bound when ye do what I say; but when ye do not what I say, ye have no promise" (D&C 82:10). When the Lord makes a deal with you, He will come through with His side of it only if you come through with yours. Your obedience determines your spiritual progress. Obedience is not simply checking off a laundry list of rules, but it is encompassed in pure, Christlike service. It's a simple equation: Obedience + Faith = Blessings.

Developing a Christlike Character

For some people the phrase "building character" carries a negative connotation (maybe because it was said so frequently in the same sentence with "pulling weeds," "dumping trash," and "cleaning toilets"), but building character is really an incredible, thrilling thing. Powerful people have depth of character. Think of Nephi. He was obedient, faithful in every moment, willing to sacrifice his life for the cause, a great leader, inspiring speaker and writer, warrior, politician, and devout reader of the works of Isaiah. Now, you tell me if that isn't interesting! Just a prophet, huh?!

The powerful words of Jesus Christ echo in our hearts: "I am." While He *is* the total of all good attributes, of all that is pure and perfect, your key to doing great things is to *become* like Him:

> Wherefore, my beloved brethren, pray unto the Father with all the energy of heart, that ye may be filled with this love, which he hath bestowed upon all who are true followers of his Son, Jesus Christ; that *ye may become* the sons of God; that when he shall appear *we shall be like him*, for we shall see him as he is; that we may have this hope; that we may be purified even as he is pure. Amen. (Moro. 7:48; italics added)

When problems come your way (and they will if they haven't already), seek a "change of heart" from the Master of spiritual heart surgeries, and ask for help to become more like Him.

In your quest to become Christlike, you may throw your arms up in despair at the sheer difficulty of it all. Stop, be patient, and change one characteristic at a time—great characters take time to develop. Just ask Ammon, Alma, Joseph, Isaiah, Paul, John, Jacob, Joseph Smith, Ezra Taft Benson, or Gordon B. Hinckley. That is, read their mission stories and see how they did it! Notice also that not one of them lost any of their individuality by following the Savior. In fact, through proper obedience to the Lord, they created their true identities.

Elder M. Russell Ballard, in his talk "The Greatest Generation of Missionaries," boldly declared:

> What we need now is *the greatest generation of missionaries in the history of the Church*. We need worthy, qualified, spiritually ener-gized missionaries who, like Helaman's 2000 stripling warriors, are "exceedingly valiant for courage, and also for strength and activity" and who are "true at all times in whatsoever thing they [are] entrusted" (Alma 53:20).
>
> Listen to those words . . . *valiant, courage, strength, active, true.* We don't need spiritually weak and semicommitted young men. We don't need you to just fill a position; we need your whole heart and soul. We need *vibrant, thinking, passionate missionaries* who know how to listen to and respond to the whisperings of the Holy Spirit. This isn't a time for spiritual weaklings. We cannot send you on a mission to be reactivated, reformed, or to receive a

testimony. We just don't have time for that. We need you to be filled with "faith, hope, charity and love, with an eye single to the glory of God" (D&C 4:5). (*Ensign*, Nov. 2002, 47)

You are expected to be one of the greatest missionaries in the history of the Church. Now is the time. There are no excuses. It's time to step up to the camera and shine. It's time to start a legacy by building the best mission and character possible.

Choose Your Character

The list below describes two very different types of missionaries. Decide which you aspire to be. (The examples are listed under "Elder." So sisters, think in terms of "Sister Babylon" or "Sister Zion.")

Elder Babylon

- Thinks about worldly things (his girl-friend, car, "life after the mission")

- Gets bored easily in the work

- Listens to investigators so they will "shut up"

- Borrows and wastes money

- Tries to dress different (crazy ties, etc.)

- Teaches whatever he feels like teaching

- Wants to baptize people for personal glory

- Criticizes the mission president and companions

- Thinks his companion should do everything

- Thinks: "What's in it for me?"

Elder Zion

- Works so hard he has no time to think about worldly things

- Is enthusiastic about the work

- Listens to the investigators out of love

- Uses the Lord's money wisely

- Dresses like a Mini-General Authority

- Teaches what the Spirit suggests

- Wants to baptize people out of love for them

- Loves the mission president and companions

- Recognizes he and his companion are a team

- Thinks: "How can I best help the investigators?"

Elder Babylon	Elder Zion
• Likes to stay up late wasting time	• Is in bed by 10:30 P.M.
• Studies the scriptures to "show people up"	• Searches the scriptures to teach with the Spirit
• Uses study time to catch up on lost sleep	• Uses study time to search and gain revelation
• Flirts with the opposite sex	• Respectfully treats others as the Savior would
• Prays monotonously	• Prays with powerful sincerity
• Sees no purpose in mission rules and disobeys	• Sees the purpose in some rules, always obeys
• Is mainly motivated by a feeling of "I have to"	• Is mainly motivated by a feeling of "I decide to"
• Has a "Let's see what happens" attitude	• Has a "Let's *make* things happen!" attitude
• Writes parents to complain and ask for money	• Writes parents to express love
• Waits for other people to talk to him first	• Talks to people about the gospel every day
• Compares himself to others	• Compares himself to himself
• Thinks everything is too hard	• Finds fun and purpose in hard work
• When on the plane home, is haunted with regrets of what could have been	• When on the plane home, is filled with joy because he worked hard to the end
• Comes home in perfect condition	• Comes home like a returning soldier
• Lives his life at home as he did on his mission	• Lives his life at home as he did on his mission
• Deters people from Christ	• Brings people to Christ

This list of characteristics is not to point out people and whisper, "Oh, he's an 'Elder Babylon,' because he . . ." Instead, it is a guide to recognize good or bad behaviors in yourself in order to make proper course corrections. I can honestly confirm that I'm not always under the heading of "Elder Zion," but I can say that by focusing my efforts on doing so I have seen significant results.

Remember that character development is a process, not a one-time event. If you don't have the attributes you want, then practice the "as if" principle and you will get them. That is, act as if you already have those attributes, and you will quickly develop them. If you don't feel at all charitable toward others right now, force yourself to show love for people today (even the ones that intensely irritate you) and pretty soon your feelings toward others will change, and loving others will come naturally.

Character is one of the only things you will ultimately take with you into the next life (see D&C 130:19–21). Develop Christlike attributes by recognizing where you are now and pushing yourself to the next level. To help you determine where you're at, take the Spiritual Power Test at the end of the chapter.

PRODUCER'S POWER TIP
"Therefore, what manner of men ought ye to be? Verily, I say unto you, even as I am" (3 Ne. 27:27).

WRITER'S CORNER
Fill out the Spiritual Power Test.

Spiritual Power Test
Write a number from 1 to 10 in each box in the first column for the level you are at *now* in each category. Fill in the second column later to measure your progress. (You might recognize these attributes as President Hinckley's Six B's.)

> **Power Meter**
> 1–3: no, not at all, or very little
> 4–7: somewhat, to a degree
> 8–10: a lot, powerfully

ATTRIBUTE	NOW	NEXT MONTH
1. Grateful		
Do I thank Heavenly Father and others daily for what I receive?	☐	☐
Do I think more about what I have than what I don't have?	☐	☐
Am I more concerned with giving than with getting?	☐	☐
Do I serve others because I really want to?	☐	☐
2. Smart		
Do I obey the Word of Wisdom?	☐	☐
Am I dedicated to constantly nourishing my mind and soul through reading faithful literature (scriptures, etc.)?	☐	☐
Do I work hard in school?	☐	☐

3. Clean

Am I committed to keeping my thoughts completely clean? ☐ ☐

Do I focus more on the spiritual than physical beauty of others? ☐ ☐

Do I "bridle my passions" so I can be "filled with love?" ☐ ☐

4. True

Am I honest in all my dealings? ☐ ☐

Do I work hard and give a solid day's work? ☐ ☐

Do I serve with all my "heart, might, mind, and strength?" ☐ ☐

Am I a faithful tithe payer? ☐ ☐

5. Humble

Do I pray sincerely every day, morning and night? ☐ ☐

Am I focused on what God wants above what I want? ☐ ☐

Do I try to "always remember" the Savior in all that I do? ☐ ☐

Am I happy to serve others? ☐ ☐

6. Prayerful

Am I committed to praying when things are going well AND poorly? ☐ ☐

Do I always have a prayer in my heart? ☐ ☐

Pick a few attributes and set specific, measurable, attainable goals and pray to develop them. Come back to the Spiritual Power Test in one month and fill in the second column, check your progress, and then set some new goals.

DIRECTOR'S ACTION
Record one to three goals to develop some attributes listed above.

Attribute	**My Goal to Develop It**
Example: Humility	*Pray for humility three times a day*
_____	_____
_____	_____
_____	_____

CHAPTER FIVE

More Spiritual Preparation:
The Power of Prayer and Scriptures

Prayer: Powerful Two-Way Communication

Your best route to a high level of spirituality and happiness is heartfelt prayer. Talk to Heavenly Father like a good friend and do it every day. Talk to the Lord as you would talk to your neighbor. Ask the Lord for the things you desire just as you would ask your neighbor for something.

Intensify your prayers; talk more clearly and specifically than you ever have to your Heavenly Father and tell Him exactly what's on your mind. He already knows what you feel right now, but He will help you best when you humble yourself before Him and ask.

Prayer is two-way communication. How would you feel if I asked you, "How was your day?" and then plugged my ears to avoid hearing your answer? It sounds absurd, yet many prayers are like that. Powerful prayers include listening. Don't listen necessarily for an audible voice, but for a feeling in your heart. The Lord tells us in Doctrine and Covenants 9:8–9:

> But, behold, I say unto you, that you must study it out in your mind; then you must ask me if it be right, and if it is right I will cause that your bosom shall burn within you; therefore, you shall feel that it is right.

> But if it be not right you shall have no such feelings, but you shall have a stupor of thought that shall cause you to forget the thing which is wrong; therefore, you cannot write that which is sacred save it be given you from me.

Heavenly Father can make your greatest vision, to become like Him, a reality. That's His job! Help Him do His job!

How can you tell if Heavenly Father is speaking to you? The scriptures and latter-day prophets give some inspiring answers.

> But behold, that which is of God inviteth and enticeth to do good continually; wherefore, every thing which inviteth and enticeth to do good, and to love God, and to serve him, is inspired of God. (Moro. 7:13)

> But the fruit of the Spirit is love, joy, peace, longsuffering, gentleness, goodness, faith, Meekness, temperance: against such there is no law. (Gal. 5:22–23)

> I will tell you in your mind and in your heart, by the Holy Ghost, which shall come upon you and which shall dwell in your heart. (D&C 8:2)

> When you feel these swelling motions, ye will begin to say within yourselves—It must needs be that this is a good seed, or that the word is good, for it beginneth to enlarge my soul; yea, it beginneth to enlighten my understanding, yea, it beginneth to be delicious to me. (Alma 32:28)

> Did I not speak peace to your mind concerning the matter? (D&C 6:23)

> That subject seems to occupy my mind, and press itself upon my feelings. (D&C 128:1)

The promise of answered prayers is the testimony of millions and of every powerful missionary. Ask Heavenly Father for a confirmation of the truths of the gospel—that Jesus is the Christ, that Joseph Smith is a prophet of God, and that the Book of Mormon is true. Seek confirmation of these and other truths and your convictions concerning the truth will become stronger. With a strong spiritual witness of the gospel, your teaching in the mission field will be powerful.

The Scriptures: Your Mission Script

In filmmaking, scripts help actors understand the role they should be playing. As you prepare for your mission, your scripts are your scriptures. They will help you understand your role as a missionary. They unlock the keys of heaven and spiritual power, by slicing through the veil and bringing you back to walk the streets of Galilee; to suit up in armor against the sinister, evil army; to stand as a witness before the wicked king who wants to take your life because of your testimony.

What is *scripture?* Scripture is what is found in the standard works (Old and New Testaments, the Book of Mormon, Doctrine and Covenants, and The Pearl of Great Price) and any other inspired words spoken by prophets. Prophets of today have given you a manual for creating a powerful mission story: the *For the Strength of Youth* pamphlet. Consult it often and you will find power to resist and overcome temptation.

Search the scriptures for a *set time* each day. Make scripture searching a habit by doing it a specific amount of time each day, preferably in the morning. As it becomes a habit, you will be empowered to overcome adversity, discern evil, and understand light and truth that will guide you and others back to Heavenly Father. Your "mission script" will be aligned with the divine script that Heavenly Father has prepared for you.

President Ezra Taft Benson counseled:

> Establish now the *daily* practice of reading the scriptures ten to fifteen minutes each day. If you do so, by the time you reach the mission field, you will have read all four of the standard works. I urge you to *read particularly the Book of Mormon* so that you can testify of its truthfulness as the Lord has directed. (*Ensign*, May 1985, 36; italics added)

Super Search versus Casual Study

What's the difference between *searching* and *studying?* If you were on a treasure island with a map looking for buried treasure, would you simply stare at the ground and *study* the "X" that marks the spot? No, when you got to the spot, (after shouting—in a raspy pirate voice—"ARRR, there be treasure here!") you would dig like a mad pirate until you found it! Of course, the scriptures contain treasures of far greater worth than gold, so *search* the scriptures! They will bless you and the people you teach.

As you search the scriptures, look for principles in the verses you read. Principles are concentrated truths that answer a variety of questions; they are "mini equations for life." Principles produce powerful results when applied correctly.

Suppose you were to look in the scriptures to understand how to partake of the sacrament. You first look in 3 Nephi 18:10–11. You find in these verses that the purpose of partaking of the sacrament is to witness to God you are willing to do His will and always remember Jesus Christ so you can have His Spirit to be with you. This could be put as an equation like this: "Partake of the Sacrament + Take upon you the name of Jesus Christ + Obey Him + Always remember Him = Have His spirit to be with you." That's the principle! Apply that principle in *any* situation, and it will create powerful results for you. Isn't that beautiful?

The scriptures have study helps, such as the footnotes, to make searching easier. Use the footnotes at the bottom of the pages to cross-reference, clarify, and add depth. Another study help is the Topical Guide. Say you want to find out more about the sacrament. You dive into the Topical Guide, and look under "Sacrament." You find scriptures like Matthew 26:26, where Christ gives the sacrament to His disciples. You write down questions and answers about this topic. For example, "How can I better prepare to partake of the sacrament?" "What is the sacrament?" and "What does the sacrament symbolize?" This is an exploration, and you are directing it. The beauty is that you head in any direction and still come up with powerful, "sure scripts."

Follow seven crucial steps as you search:

> 1. **Ask.** Start your search session by asking Heavenly Father to help you understand. The great promise of the Lord is "ask and ye shall receive; knock, and it shall be opened unto you" (D&C 4:7).

> 2. **Search.** Search the scriptures for *specific* principles to apply now to your own life. One way to help your search be more

meaningful is to put your own name in the scriptures and watch how Jesus Christ literally speaks to *you* (see D&C 18:35–36). For example: "I, [your name], having been born of goodly parents . . ." (1 Ne. 1:1).

3. Ponder. Think deeply about how you can put what you have read into practice. You might ponder on one scripture for hours. The key is to pull out *principles* from the mere *details* of the scriptures. There are details, like the fact that Nephi was in Jerusalem trying to get the plates and wasn't sure exactly how he was going to do it, but he trusted the Lord. Then there are principles: When I am in situations when I don't know exactly what to do, I can put my full trust in the Lord and obey Him, and be blessed. Principles will powerfully change the lives of you, your investigators, and members on your mission.

4. Memorize. Memorize scriptures that teach specific principles. The more scriptures you can have in your heart, the better off you will be. If you memorize a scripture a day, you can have several, even hundreds with you by the time you reach the mission field! When you store up truth in your mind, the Lord will gladly give it to you in the moments you need it, particularly when you're teaching that investigator who has the tough questions about life.

5. Write Down. Keep a notebook or personal journal where you write down what the Lord teaches you. This shows the Lord you are interested in what He tells you, and it helps you remember promptings and the things you learn. You can also prepare outlines to help you teach doctrine. Write down a summary with related scriptures on a given topic. If your topic were the Restoration, you could include details about how prophets have been called, the Apostasy, the Reformation, the vision of Joseph Smith, and the coming forth of the Book of Mormon. Write your outlines as if you were going to teach them to a specific person (an investigator friend, a family member, etc.) or group of people (a family, a congregation, other missionaries, etc.). Keep a file of your outlines, *Ensign* articles, and other notes you've written so you can refer back to them in times of difficulty, or when a tough investigator question arises. These will come in handy when you are called on to speak or teach a principle on your mission with only a moment's notice.

6. Thank. Give the Lord credit for discoveries you receive through His spirit. Thank Him for what He teaches you. This shows Him your gratitude. Some missionaries mistakenly believe that whatever they get out of scripture study is a result of their own smarts.

7. Teach. Once you have received the word of the Lord, you have the wonderful opportunity to share it with others. Share what you learn with friends, family, and anybody you can find. Teach others and you will create experiences that set the course for a powerful mission, and repeating what you know increases your own retention of the doctrine. So, whenever you learn a new, powerful doctrine, find someone to share it with as soon as possible and watch how it changes you and them. This is essential if you are to become an Ammon- or Nephi-like servant of the Lord.

Search first, *then* teach. The Lord's admonition is clear: "Seek not to declare my word, but first seek to obtain my word, and then shall your tongue be loosed; then, if you desire, you shall have my Spirit and my word, yea, the power of God unto the convincing of men" (D&C 11:21). He also instructed: "Neither take ye thought beforehand what ye shall say; but treasure up in your minds continually the words of life, and it shall be given you in the very hour that portion that shall be meted unto every man" (D&C 84:85).

The sons of Mosiah were such powerful instruments in the Lord's hands because they seriously searched the holy scriptures *before* they served the Lord as missionaries. Before sharing the word, they obtained it.

And they had waxed strong in the knowledge of the truth; for they were men of a *sound understanding* and they had *searched* the scriptures diligently, that they might know the word of God. But this is not all; they had given themselves to *much prayer*, and fasting; therefore they had the spirit of prophecy, and the spirit of revelation, and when they taught, *they taught with power and authority of God*. (Alma 17:2–3; italics added)

Constant scripture searching will give you a spiritual edge that few people have. Like recharging a battery will give it strength to run for a long time, scripture reading will energize you to face and overcome difficult tasks on a daily basis.

Never let scripture searching fall at the mercy of less important things. Some missionaries will focus study time on things like listening to music, reading other books, sleeping, or even teaching people instead of searching the scriptures. Walking outside to teach others without having first prepared yourself through powerful study is like walking into a war without any armor versus an army of super-prepared, armored warriors (the Lamanites knew what that was like, and it didn't turn out very well for them). So, search!

PRODUCER'S POWER TIP:
President Hinckley stated:

> Without reservation I promise you that if you will prayerfully read the Book of Mormon, regardless of how many times you have previously read it, there will come into your heart . . . the Spirit of the Lord. There will come a strengthened resolution to walk in obedience to his commandments, and there will come a stronger testimony of the living reality of the Son of God. . . . Those who have read it prayerfully have grown under its power. (*Teachings of Gordon B. Hinckley* [1998], 41)

WRITER'S CORNER
What are some gospel doctrines that you might have a difficult time with or be uncomfortable teaching right now?

_____

_____

_____

_____

How can you prepare to teach those doctrines powerfully?

_____

_____

_____

_____

DIRECTOR'S ACTION
Prayerfully search the scriptures, particularly the Book of Mormon, every day. Seek the Spirit as you do and write an outline each week on a specific doctrine (the Restoration, the Plan of Salvation, the Atonement, etc.), and then teach it to someone you know. Look for opportunities to team up with the missionaries in your ward or stake and teach investigators whenever you can.

CHAPTER SIX

Powerful Moral Preparation

The Lord needs missionaries who are morally prepared. Joseph F. Smith said:

> We want young men . . . who have kept themselves unspotted from the world. . . . Where you get men like this to preach the gospel to the world, whether they know much to begin with or not, the Lord will put his Spirit into their hearts, and he will crown them with intelligence and power to save the souls of men. (*Gospel Doctrine*, 5th ed. [1939], 356)

The more Satan can get someone to lose focus on the mission, the merrier he is. The more you let him sneak into your life through the worldly, sensual ways, the more your effectiveness as an instrument in God's hands will diminish.

President Spencer W. Kimball described Satan's tactics for getting you to make wrong choices:

> Whoever said that sin was not fun? Whoever claimed that Lucifer was not handsome, persuasive, easy, friendly? Sin is attractive and desirable. Transgression wears elegant gowns and sparkling apparel. It is highly perfumed; it has attractive features, a soft voice. It is found in educated circles and sophisticated groups. It provides sweet and comfortable luxuries. Sin is easy and has a big company of pleasant companions. It promises immunity from restrictions, temporary freedoms. It can momentarily satisfy hunger, thirst, desire, urges, passions, wants without

immediately paying the price. But, it begins tiny and grows to monumental proportions—drop by drop, inch by inch. (*Faith Precedes the Miracle* [1972], 229)

Avoid the negative effects of moral sin by keeping high standards in dating, your entertainment choices, and your thoughts.

Romance or Adventure?

Satan would have you believe that you should have everything *now*. A lasting relationship with a spouse, for example, is a great thing to have, but the prophets have said that it should only be developed at the right time; for young men who are able to serve a mission that time is *after* they come home honorably.

The adversary tries to destroy and weaken our ability to help others. He wants you to believe that you should become emotionally and physically involved with someone before your mission, because he says "you'll be married anyway after your mission."

There is a very slim chance that person will actually wait for you. Besides, you'll have plenty of time to go spouse shopping at the right time and right place, but not before your mission. After all, what part of a movie would you rather watch first, the adventure or the romance? Adventure first!

Entertainment: Watch Out!

President Gordon B. Hinckley proclaimed:

> I am always curious when individuals insist that what they watch . . . doesn't affect them. . . . Are we really to believe that hours, leading to years, of television viewing will not affect attitudes about everything from family life to appropriate sexual relations? (*Standing for Something* [2000], 36)

Sometimes people get uptight about their selection of entertainment. They say: "It's my choice!" "I can watch what I want." Of course, they are absolutely right. However, the question isn't about personal choice, it's about right and wrong. If the Savior walked into the theater or TV room and sat down right next to you, would *He* stay and watch? If not, it's time to change—*right now*. Be grateful that the Lord, who is infinitely wise, and has power and dominion over millions of worlds, with infinite children, is interested and deeply concerned with what *you* listen to and watch, how *you* dress, and how *you* treat others.

Recreation can be good, when it is not in excess. Deep down, we all know the difference between when we're being entertained with purpose, and when we're just using time to turn our brain into Jell-O. Compare using a half an hour a day to watch some favorite television sitcom versus reading the scriptures. It doesn't even come close! And, yet, a lot of people sit and watch away their lives, living someone else's life on TV instead of going out and experiencing real life on their own big screen.

Why not spend the time watching TV or movies to create your own story? Just as the idle mind is the devil's workshop, the *active* mind is God's workshop. Socialize, serve others, or write a book, a poem, or a movie script about your own life experiences. After all, you and I will be judged for how we used our time here on earth. Your real adventure, your greatest drama, and your funniest comedy are waiting to be discovered right in your own life.

With Church standards, established by prophets (and God Himself), people sometimes think: "I agree with all of them except that *one*." That is how they label their favorite sin—be it dating before the age of sixteen, viewing pornography, or engaging in inappropriate physical intimacy. You should be above that. You, like Adam, recognize that every commandment has a purpose behind it, known by the Lord, even though you might not understand it completely right now (see Moses 5:6). You understand that the small decisions of today literally dictate your tomorrow. You want an inspiring, clean life story, so direct your mission with that end in mind.

Prophets warn against pornography. It may seem like something small to disobey this counsel, but a virus is something small too—and how much damage can a small, practically invisible virus do? Just like a virus can kill its unsuspecting victim in a very short time, disobedience to God's prophets can seriously damage or even paralyze you spiritually. It may be slow, "inch by inch," but that is how Satan works. If he can get you to slip up once, it will be that much easier for him next time, and so on.

It may sound like leaders and parents repeat the same talks over and over about dating and sexual purity—there is a reason for the repetition. A young man once rebelled against such counsel and even bragged about how he destroyed his *For the Strength of Youth* pamphlet. Now, consequently his life is reflective of that attitude. He went on a mission, but shamefully returned home after a short time and has lived an unhappy, unfulfilled life. Disobedience to the prophets never brings happiness.

Sometimes the people around us encourage us to do things we know are wrong, or they make it difficult to avoid bad choices. One missionary offers the following perspective: "First, change your friends [if they are not the right kind of friends]. It is hard to do, but it will save your life. Trust me. I started hanging out with two of my Church friends instead of my 'thug' friends and it made all the difference. You need to realize who is good for you and who isn't."

Directing Your "Actors": Thoughts about Your Thoughts

Moral preparation is more than just not *doing* bad things. Bad actions are the trees that come from the *roots* of bad thoughts.

King Benjamin cautioned:

> But this much I can tell you, that if ye do not watch yourselves, and your thoughts, and your words, and your deeds, and observe the commandments of God, and continue in the faith of what ye have heard concerning the coming of our Lord, even unto the end of your lives, ye must perish. And now, O man, remember, and perish not. (Mosiah 4:30)

Keeping your thoughts clean will keep your actions clean, which will keep your life clean, which will help your investigators make their thoughts clean, which will keep their actions clean, which will keep their lives clean and lead you both back to Heavenly Father. Are you confused now, or do you see the power of just one thought? *One thought* could be the difference in saving a soul. Struggling with your thoughts is normal and necessary, but letting your mind drift or feeding bad thoughts can destroy you.

Thoughts will literally dictate your destiny. You tell your thoughts what to do, not the other way around. Some people excuse filthy thoughts with "I can't help it," not recognizing they are the directors of their own lives. If the director doesn't believe he has any power, then a mission story is truly doomed.

As your own director, guide your *thoughts*. Your thoughts are your actors. You determine your thoughts. Satan can influence you, but only God can read your thoughts. Spencer W. Kimball powerfully proclaimed:

> How could a person possibly become what he is *not* thinking? Nor is any thought, when persistently entertained, too small to have its effect. The "divinity that shapes our ends" is indeed in ourselves. (*The Miracle of Forgiveness* [1981], 104–105)

Whenever you have a bad thought, take a "director cut" and don't just try to destroy the bad thought, replace it with a good one. The best thought that will eliminate all doubt and fear, erase all filth, and bring you consecutive victories forever is Jesus Christ. Think of His life, how He loved and served people, and the experiences when you have felt closest to Him. Remember the promise that as you "always remember Him," you will "have His spirit to be with [you]." Believe it. Live it. It is real.

When Satan comes tempting you, remember who you are. Knowing that you are a son or daughter of God, just like Jesus Christ is, helps you make wise decisions. Moses did, when he declared to that father of lies, "Who art thou? For behold, I am a son of God, in the similitude of his Only Begotten; and where is thy glory, that I should worship thee?" (Moses 1:13).

Another method is to simply tell Satan to go to you know where. Moses did something like this when he boldly stated, "Depart from me, Satan, for this one God only will I worship, which is the God of glory" (Moses 1:20). General Authorities also suggest memorizing favorite hymns to sing when bad thoughts come into your mind. This works. So, when your actors (or thoughts) are "acting up," think hymns.

Be a Captain or "Miss" Moroni

In "The Greatest Generation of Missionaries," Elder Ballard counseled:

> Resolve and commit to yourselves and to God that from this moment forward you will strive diligently to keep your heart, hands, and mind pure and unsullied from any kind of moral transgression. Resolve to avoid pornography as you would avoid the most insidious disease, for that is precisely what it is. Resolve to completely abstain from tobacco, alcohol, and illegal drugs. Resolve to be honest. Resolve to be good citizens and to abide by the laws of the land in which you live. Resolve that . . . you will never defile your body or use language that is vulgar and unbecoming to a bearer of the priesthood. (*Ensign*, Nov. 2002, 47)

As you carefully keep God's commandments and prepare spiritually for your mission, others will want to follow. They will think: "I want to be like him (or her); I want to be great." Be like Paul the Apostle, who said: "Wherefore I beseech you, be ye followers of me" (1 Cor. 4:16). His example was so strong that he could powerfully, and without hesitation, invite others to follow him. Whose example was Paul following? Christ's, of course. So, you basically are saying to others "Follow me as I follow Jesus. If I slip a little, help me get back up."

One missionary, Jeff, inspired others to go on missions. He did what was right. He was nice to others. He treated his parents with respect and love. He didn't get into trouble. He was a hard-working Boy Scout, and later became an awesome missionary. Most importantly, he represented Jesus Christ well. In watching him, others decided to serve powerful missions *like he did*.

Whether you realize it or not, many young people are watching the big screen of your life. What will you do? How will you react in a tough situation, when you are tempted to cheat on a test, or invited to take a drink or a smoke or to look at some pornographic material? Stand for something! Be an example! As you keep high moral standards, you will be an example and an inspiration to others.

PRODUCER'S POWER TIP
"Let no man despise thy youth; but be thou an example of the believers, in word, in conversation, in charity, in spirit, in faith, in purity" (1 Tim. 4:12).

WRITER'S CORNER
Why is moral preparation important to you?

_____

_____

_____

_____

_____

DIRECTOR'S ACTION
Commit today to live a clean life and participate only in entertainment and dating that is approved by the Savior and His servants. Encourage others to do the same.

CHAPTER SEVEN

Powerful Physical Preparation

Why is physical preparation so important for a mission? First, missionary work is physically challenging. While there are some things you can't anticipate, you can focus on areas of your life you *can* control to prepare physically for mission life. Second, as a missionary, you will personally challenge people to give up certain behaviors—anything from chastity issues to Word of Wisdom problems like smoking and drinking. To challenge such individuals with power, you need to have taken important preliminary steps in self-mastery.

If spiritual progress is a ladder, then physical self-mastery is the very first rung. Can you imagine someone who sets a goal to say their prayers early every morning, but can't get up to offer them? Self-mastery is your starting point for personal progress.

Sleep: Early to Bed, Early to Rise

Self-mastery includes getting to bed early and getting up early. At this point you might be thinking, "Ouch—did he have to mention that?" or "I get to bed early. 1:00 A.M. is early." Well, getting to bed early is what you'll be doing as a full-time missionary for two years, and hopefully for the rest of your life. Get adequate rest by getting to bed early if you don't already. Powerful blessings are reserved for those who are awake during the early hours of the day. The Lord states, "Cease to be idle; . . . cease to sleep longer than is needful; retire to thy bed early, that ye may not be weary; arise early, that your bodies and your minds may be invigorated" (D&C 88:124).

Some future missionaries think, "Yeah, I'll just start getting to bed and up early when I get out there." That may sound fine, but you'll prevent a lot of headaches by applying the principle *now*. It's always better to start new habits TODAY.

Food, Glorious Food

Watch what you eat. Besides avoiding obvious bad stuff (leather, tires, etc.), *eat right* from now on. Stay away from too much junk food. The term "you are what you eat" is true in how it relates to your physical appearance. If you sit around all day, watching TV and eating Twinkies, you'll start to look like one—puffy, fluffy, and creamy. Eat a balanced diet and you will grow stronger. Keep a good balance of the four food groups, and especially eat fruits and vegetables (for some reason those little, yummy guys often get so lonely).

Try new foods before you go on your mission. Experiment with your mom's meat loaf casserole or whatever it is you don't think you like—it will help you be more willing to accept food you might get in a foreign country (like Texas). In my mission, I partook of cow stomach, intestines, chicken guts, and little, furry hamsters. They really didn't taste all that bad—but I was able to eat them without any serious problems because I had tried new foods before my mission, including sushi (a Japanese food consisting of uncooked fish). Keep a sense of humor and a willingness to accept new things. This will help you win the hearts of investigators and members on your mission.

Learn to cook different foods. You might have to cook on your mission, and so you will want to be able to make foods that are not only edible, but good (more than just peanut butter and jelly sandwiches).

Physical Fitness and Hygiene

Gain greater control over your body through physical fitness. Keep physically fit. Play sports. If you don't like sports, set up a physical fitness program. You could do push-ups or sit-ups, jogging, biking, or even walking. Find out from your parents, doctor, or coach what exercises would be best for you.

As you exercise, try to do more each time than you did previously. For example, if you do one more sit-up a day than the day previous, you could do thirty sit-ups by the end of the month. Constantly lifting the expectation for yourself will increase your strength and build your system. Use wisdom. Avoid overworking yourself or straining your muscles by forgetting to stretch and properly warm up.

Those who avoid physical fitness or procrastinate it find system malfunctions in their body. Maintain physical fitness by exercising in some way at least a half an hour a day, three days a week.

Practice cleanliness and hygiene. Hygiene includes showering often (this one's a biggie), brushing your teeth, and keeping your room clean. You don't want to be sick on your mission. Cleanliness *is* next to godliness.

Set powerful physical fitness goals. Consider what you want to achieve in physical fitness. What's your goal? Do you just want to stay healthy? If so, that is excellent—focus on achieving that. Do you want to *increase* your physical strength and stamina? Do you want to prepare for a triathlon or some other type of physical competition, like playing on a sports team at school?

One last thing to remember is that service to the Lord in and of itself invigorates you. The Lord declared, "For whoso is faithful unto the obtaining these two priesthoods of which I have spoken, and the magnifying their calling, are sanctified by the Spirit unto the renewing of their bodies" (D&C 84:33). I have seen this promise fulfilled powerfully in the lives of many missionaries. Those who "put their shoulder to the wheel" are strengthened and made fit to face the challenges of missionary work.

PRODUCER'S POWER TIP

Remember the promised blessings for keeping the Word of Wisdom: "And all saints who remember to keep and do these sayings, walking in obedience to the commandments, shall receive health in their navel and marrow to their bones; and shall find wisdom and great treasures of knowledge, even hidden treasures; and shall run and not be weary, and shall walk and not faint" (D&C 89:18–20).

WRITER'S CORNER

How do you imagine the most fit, healthy, and mission-prepared you?

_____

_____

_____

_____

_____

What can you do to become that way now?

_____

_____

_____

_____

DIRECTOR'S ACTION

Commit to sleeping right, eating right, and exercising for a half an hour at least three times a week. Adapt your health program to best fit your needs and watch how it affects your positive outlook and spirit.

CHAPTER EIGHT

Powerful Financial Preparation

Prepare financially for your mission. Your parents may pitch in or even pay for it all, but you should still save for your mission. It is a sad thing when a young man hasn't worked or saved at all for his mission simply because he expected his parents to do it all. That young man will not experience that special feeling of saving for something so worthwhile.

Try to save a big part or all of what is needed for your mission. With each paycheck you receive, you can increase your savings dramatically. All it takes is a trip to the local bank. This will be well worth it. Always remember that a mission is an investment, not a cost. Set priorities with your money, and discipline yourself to use it wisely and to save appropriately.

Get a job, *especially* during the summer. In whatever you do to financially prepare, work hard. A mission is work. Prepare well for it, and you will be better off. For some missionaries, knocking doors selling products, doing yard-work, washing windows, mowing lawns, and doing construction helped them prepare for their mission. It really doesn't matter what type of work you do (as long as it's ethical). Also, don't work on Sundays. You will be blessed with spiritual power if you don't.

Financial preparation and working hard go hand in hand. By working hard, you will become a truly powerful servant of the Lord—respected and loved by your mission president and fellow missionaries. You will be empowered to face difficult days that lie ahead of you. One of the craziest things on your mission is to experience moments when you are physically drained, overworked, overstressed, and fatigued, yet simultaneously having the most fun of your life!

Elder Allen, a cowboy mission companion of mine from Idaho, knew how to work—he was an "Elder Ammon." He *loved* hard work; it was deep in his soul. He walked so fast to every single appointment, he never had time to whine or complain about how hard it was. He inspired hundreds of missionaries to be faithful and to serve with all their heart, might, mind, and strength. What Elder Allen did wasn't simply because of what he learned on his mission; he had learned to value hard work long before he hit the field.

Ezra Taft Benson, in the September 1990 *Ensign*, stated:

> If [you] want to keep the Spirit, [you] must work. There is no greater exhilaration or satisfaction than to know, after a hard day of work, that [you] have done [your] best.

> I have often said that one of the greatest secrets of missionary work is work! If a missionary works, he will get the Spirit; if he gets the Spirit, he will teach by the Spirit; and if he teaches by the Spirit, he will touch the hearts of the people and he will be happy. Work, work, work—there is no satisfactory substitute, especially in missionary work. (6–7)

Financial preparation includes paying an honest tithe and focusing your work efforts on what is most important. Elder Ballard has encouraged those preparing for missions to commit to "working and putting part of [their] earnings in a savings account" and "paying a full and honest tithing" (*Ensign*, Nov. 2002, 48).

In addition to working hard, saving money, and paying tithing, practice thriftiness. As you do, remember that the key to financial success is to spend *less* than you earn. Don't waste money on toys that will not be of any worth to you once you hit the mission field. Make a budget each month and determine how much you will spend in different categories. Set a category for "Mission" and start filling it up.

PRODUCER'S POWER TIP
Elder Victor L. Brown said, "I have concluded that if we meet today's problems with adequate preparation, there will be no need for panic preparation" (*Ensign*, Nov. 1982, 79).

WRITER'S CORNER
What are some ways you can prepare financially for your mission?

_____
_____
_____
_____

Why is hard work so important in missionary work?

_____
_____
_____
_____

How much money will you save for your mission? _____

How much per month? _____

What jobs will you do to earn this money?

_____
_____
_____
_____

DIRECTOR'S ACTION
Write down a specific plan of action to prepare financially, including a budget for how much you will save each month. Plan how much you will earn and spend each month and follow up weekly.

CHAPTER NINE

Powerful Mental Preparation

Ezra Taft Benson, in the May 1985 *Ensign*, said:

> Prepare yourselves mentally. A mission requires a great deal of mental preparation. You must [master] missionary discussions, memorize scriptures, and oftimes learn a new language. The discipline to do this is learned in your early years. (26)

As a student at Brigham Young University, I was walking to class one day and noticed a large group of people. Upon approaching, I saw President Gordon B. Hinckley, about to speak at the library dedication. I quickly found a spot to sit, thirty feet from the prophet! As I listened to his message, I felt a confirmation of his divine calling.

President Hinckley spoke on the importance of getting an education, continually pursuing knowledge in good books, and developing our minds for the Lord's purposes. After the dedication, he exited toward where I was standing. I awaited some special counsel from this wonderful prophet. After cordially escorting his wife into the car, he turned to us and said with a giant, prophet-size smile: "Be Smart!"

What does it mean to *be smart*? To be smart is to develop yourself mentally. Work hard to get good grades, an education, and training. Read good books, and learn a new language. Many missionaries who have studied a language in high school have been called to missions to speak that very same language. Education opens doors for you to bless and influence people.

You progress in quantum leaps as you see the adventure in applying new principles. Your mind expands, your ability to achieve increases, and you even prepare yourself for the next life (see D&C 130:19–21).

And as all have not faith, seek ye diligently and teach one
another words of wisdom; yea, seek ye out of the best books
words of wisdom; seek learning, even by study and also by faith.
(D&C 88:118)

Find subjects that interest you, and study them. If you like
science, read about it in books! If you enjoy history, read books about
history! If you like mysteries, film, art, math, or engineering, read
about it in books! Challenge yourself by reading a set amount of new
books per week, month, and year.

Having grown up in school and received book reports and assign-
ments, you might feel that books are a form of punishment. That's
where imagination comes in. If something is boring to you—be it
science, geography, or economics, you can actually psyche yourself
into liking the subject. You've got to want to, however.

Another important opportunity for exercising those mental
muscles is school. It is possible to cruise along in a vegetable-like state
without ever really pounding the books. Instead, go for academic
excellence. Set specific goals for your desired grade point average. Talk
to your teachers and let them know that you are interested in learning
and achieving good grades. Do all of your homework ASAP. Schedule
a few hours each day at a time when your brain is functioning best in a
place where you can focus (safety tip: not in front of the TV or in a
warm bed!). Finally, pray for the Lord's help in your studies, and let
the Spirit teach you.

Talents

Most people have determined they are not good at something
simply because someone once told them they weren't. You may have
once drawn a picture that your first grade teacher hated, or tried to
play the piano and created a sound like the piano was dying, or acted
in a play and blew your line. So, you may be haunted by a memory,
telling yourself, "I am bad at _____" or "I am not a good _____."

To become effective with a certain talent, have a positive experience at it. Prepare yourself for a positive experience in some talent
through *intense* preparation. Program yourself to be awesome at that
particular thing through practice, and you will continually draw upon

the positive experiences that you create. You will create your own "success cycle." Apply this to drawing, science, math, public speaking, or any field of endeavor. Some people are simply more naturally gifted in particular areas, but you can develop talents that perhaps were previously invisible to you.

Many people say things like, "I'd love to learn to play the guitar," but they never learn simply because they don't put in the time necessary to practice. My good friend (in fact, he's my brother) Ed taught himself to play the guitar. He wasn't born a guitarist, but he learned through daily practice. Set goals to develop talents. Use your talents in the mission field to bless lives—don't bury them.

In some missions, you can establish programs to teach English classes, art, finance, or some other talent. As you help others develop their talents, they will be that much more willing to hear your beautiful, life-changing message. I know of one missionary who established an English-teaching program in his mission that became a major success. The classes were so well organized and effective that people flocked to participate in them. They listened, learned English, and then quickly became curious about these men in white shirts, sporting black name tags, teaching the classes. Their curiosity sparked interest and conversion. To them, it was a privilege to take the English classes, and even more of a privilege to hear the discussions from the missionaries.

Develop your mind, and you will discover newfound wisdom and power in your teaching adventures.

PRODUCER'S POWER TIP
President Gordon B. Hinckley, in the September 1996 *Ensign*, shared: "Make something of your lives. It isn't enough just to exist. You must equip yourselves so that you can make a contribution to the society of which we are a part. . . . Be hungry for education. Sacrifice for it, work for it, plan for it, and do it" (77).

WRITER'S CORNER
What are some mental mission preparation goals you would like to set in your life right now? (increase GPA, develop new talents, read certain books, study a new language, etc.)

_____

_____

_____

_____

_____

_____

How will developing your mind prepare you for your mission?

_____

_____

_____

_____

_____

In what other ways do you plan on developing your mind to meet the task of missionary work?

_____

_____

_____

_____

DIRECTOR'S ACTION

Set aside any pride, prejudice, or laziness that might be holding you back from accomplishing amazing mental feats in your life. Equip yourself now for your adventures in teaching by learning from the great men and women who have gone before. Put yourself in their shoes (or sandals) and watch yourself change into a Christlike, powerful servant of the Lord. Create a mental preparation plan, including specific goals for what talents you will develop, what books you will have read before your mission, what academic achievements you will accomplish, etc.

CHAPTER TEN

Powerful Social Preparation

Before my mission, especially during high school, I had a hard time communicating with others—when spoken to I would often mumble, get fidgety, and then stare at the floor. I will never forget how reading the account of Enoch changed me. Enoch also had weaknesses—particularly in communicating with others.

In the May 1981 *New Era*, Elder Neal A. Maxwell emphasized:

> When the prophet Enoch was called, he wondered why and said, "I . . . am but a lad, and all the people hate me; for I am slow of speech" (Moses 6:31). Yet Enoch knew that in responding to God the test is not our capability but our availability. Enoch kept the commandments and trusted in the Lord's vision of his possibilities, going on to become the builder of the greatest city of all time. . . . Your personal possibilities, not for status and position but for *service* to God and mankind, are immense, if you will but trust the Lord to lead you from what you are to what you have the power to become. (4)

If you struggle to communicate with others, there are things you can do to help yourself improve. Go out of your way to show love and create lasting friendships. Join clubs, or get involved in sports or other activities that bring you together with others and create opportunities to interact. Learn to communicate with others by doing it. Have a genuine sense of humor, and be an interesting person by sharing your hobbies, hopes, and dreams. People like to be around positive friends who radiate values centered on Christ. People like friends who stand up for good, and who really care about them. Don't be shy, and don't be afraid to serve others in new, out-of-your-comfort zone ways.

In the same talk, Elder Maxwell said:

> Believe in yourselves not only for what you now are, but for what you have the possibilities to become!

> Trust yourselves to the Lord who sees the end from the beginning—and all that is in between! He sees you as you are but also what you may become! Meanwhile, do not let your present feelings of inadequacy keep you from growing or responding to your challenges. Do not let the pressures of time cause you to make choices that will damage your eternity. (4)

Listening

Help others see *their* personal potential. Take a special interest in them—see things from their point of view. You don't necessarily have to agree with them, but you will show them love by manifesting your desire to understand their position. This is empathic listening, and it is a priceless missionary skill.

People naturally need to be heard and understood—it's like water for thirsty hearts. Excellent missionaries try to understand the hearts of others the way Jesus Christ knows us. As the scriptures say, Jesus Christ is the "life and the light." He really is. You must also be a "light" for others. Be excited when you speak to someone, and they will likely become excited too. Be apathetic and others will respond likewise. Make a good impression with your firm handshake, smile, and confident speech.

Heart Preparation

Remember names. That may sound easy, but after meeting hundreds and thousands of new people, you will easily forget names. Look at people when you first meet them and repeat their name three times in your conversation with them, and you will remember it. People love to hear their own name—it's the sweetest sound to them.

Learn and remember birthdays, family information, personal dreams, and aspirations. Express intense interest in peoples' lives. Treat people like you've known them for years, and they will likely treat you that way. When missionaries do this, they can impact people eternally. Have you ever met a General Authority? They are awesome examples of missionary work. Why? They treat you like a true brother or sister, like Jesus Christ treats you.

Be authentic. *Authentic* comes from a Greek word meaning *author.* Be the real and the best you. Create your destiny by effectively and originally writing your life. By being authentic in your relationships, your influence will automatically expand into others' lives. Your mission story will beam with truth, happiness, and success.

We love Jesus Christ because He loved us first (see 1 Jn. 4:10, 19). You must first love others. You've got to give to get, especially in missionary work. The more love you share with people, the more personal your message becomes. People respond to love. You may have your heart broken when someone rejects this precious message, but what joy you'll feel when the chosen hear and obey.

It's an interesting thing, but people value your message only in proportion to how much love you show to them. I'm going to repeat that principle because it is so vital: *People value your message only in proportion to how much love you show to them.* Love is *the* great motivator. It is manifest in showing interest in another, teaching truth, and building through compliments. Focus on others, not on yourself, and you will find they will be extremely interested in what you have to say. Seek the guidance of the Spirit. Remember, too, this is an adventure!

There is no greater adventure than to explore the lives of others. But you should never try to force or manipulate others to change their lives. Think of it: Someone stepping on the set of another director who is directing his own movie, and the actor yelling, "You're doing it all wrong! You idiot! Give me the script. Let me show you how to do this!" It sounds a little crazy, but it's exactly what happens when we try to force others to live like us.

Your job is simple: Love others and *inspire* them to follow the example of Jesus Christ. So, you need to be directing a powerful mission story yourself, otherwise they will not follow you (or, even worse, they will follow you down the wrong road). Jesus Christ led others in such a convincing, powerful way because He created a life story that was impeccable. People could follow Him without any qualms. They knew His character because He consistently showed love, kindness, pure service, charity, and faith. In *Teachings of Gordon B. Hinckley*, President Hinckley expressed the importance of heartfelt teaching:

> We must strengthen ourselves and our people to get our teachers to speak out of their hearts rather than out of their books, to communicate their love for the Lord and this precious work, and somehow it will catch fire in the hearts of those they teach. ([2000], 619–20)

Be a Hero

Each person has his or her story to tell, as you have your story. People are looking for a hero in *you*. Missionaries want someone to follow. Disciples of Christ and investigators who don't know anything about Jesus Christ need you as an example.

You don't have to, and really can't, be Ammon, President Hinckley, or your bishop. You can only be you. But be the best you; the most perfect you can be. It's time to step up. Put your pride, weaknesses, and shortcomings on the line and put the Lord first in *all* things. You are His first string. He is depending on you to pull through for Him in the last of the final seconds of the biggest heart-pounding adventure in history. And the clock is ticking!

My sister, Marianne, is one of my greatest heroes. She is a spiritual fighter. She was born with cerebral palsy, a handicap that affects normal activities. She could have decided with the challenges presented her "I was born to fail!" but she has never, ever given up. Instead, she expresses gratitude to Heavenly Father, and humbly serves others. She has gone to college and served an honorable full-time mission. By overcoming difficult circumstances always with a grateful attitude, she has inspired many people to be more Christlike.

Never underestimate your influence. Help others direct their life stories by first focusing on yours, then helping them in kindness. You will be in a position to inspire. You must represent Jesus Christ so when people think of you they will think of Him—because you represent Him so well. There is love, truth, and light in you. "Let your light so shine . . ."

PRODUCER'S POWER TIP

Joseph Smith declared: "Let every selfish feeling be not only buried, but annihilated, and let love to God and man predominate, and reign triumphant in every mind" (*Teachings of the Prophet Joseph Smith*, sel. Joseph Fielding Smith [1976], 178–79).

WRITER'S CORNER

How do you think Heavenly Father feels about you? Why?

_____

_____

_____

_____

_____

_____

_____

_____

How can you help others feel Heavenly Father's great love for them?

_____

_____

_____

_____

_____

_____

_____

_____

DIRECTOR'S ACTION

The next time someone does something that might trigger anger in your heart (e.g., cut you off, headbutt you, call you a mean name), think about Heavenly Father's love for that person. Pray for more charity in your life, and then share it with others.

CHAPTER ELEVEN

What You Need to Know about the Field

As a teacher at the MTC (Missionary Training Center), I discovered some powerful pointers that will help you know a little better what to expect in the mission field. Consider this chapter a "sneak preview" of the adventure that is to come. Of course, I couldn't possibly stuff *everything* there is to know into one chapter, but I sure tried. Read on about learning the language, working with companions, helping the mission president, conversion, difficult questions, and teaching with power. If you've still got questions after this, see the appendix in the back, "Answers to Big Questions."

Learning a New Language

You may be called to a place where the people speak a different language. This can either be seen as a blessing or a challenge, or both. For new missionaries in the MTC, this is one of their biggest concerns. They want to know when they will be able to speak well enough for others to understand. They work and pray hard to learn their new language. Something starts to happen as they work and pray and that is the miracle of the gift of tongues.

To learn a language quickly and well, read the Book of Mormon in that language, aloud to yourself for at least fifteen minutes each day. This helps you learn pronunciation, grammar, and vocabulary—to speak like a native in a very short time. It is the power of the Book of Mormon applied to language learning.

If you will be learning a new language, your biggest key is to speak the language as much as possible and learn to teach the basic doctrines so you can defend the kingdom. Some missionaries, when they get to the MTC or field look for every opportunity to speak English, and they offend people by speaking just English to others, because the people don't understand (and offending people isn't a positive missionary quality). In the MTC there is a program that encourages the speaking of the language you are learning. Do it and you will be blessed with the gift of tongues. You will receive the confidence you need to teach with power.

Solving Problems in Companionships

One of my companions was a feisty, five-foot-nothing, loving Peruvian—a strong-spirited trainer who pushed me to teach well. I struggled with the language. I could say "Hola" and some other phrases, but most of what came out of my mouth sounded like telephone static. But I wanted to serve the Lord in the very best way I could. To do this, I knew that I would have to be 100 percent obedient to the rules to have the Spirit.

As time went by, my companion and I worked hard at teaching investigators and activating less-active members. We worked together, but I noticed we needed to be even more obedient to small rules. After all, didn't we come on a mission to be obedient to the Lord? I was a little scared to approach him with how I felt. One night, our conversations about obedience came to a climax. I expressed my desire to be 100 percent obedient to all of the mission rules and obedient to the Spirit. Tears of understanding were shed (big boys DO cry), and we both felt the Spirit very strongly as we prayed together and communicated openly and honestly. We decided to be 100 percent obedient.

With companions, your best guide is the Spirit. Communicate with love. Smile a lot. Share your real feelings with him or her. Pray together. Study together. Talk together about the people you are teaching and how you can help them. Some of your most precious mission moments will be found right in the very apartment you live in, with your companion.

People respond to love. Joseph Smith confirmed:

> Nothing is so much calculated to lead people to forsake sin as to
> take them by the hand, and watch over them with tenderness.
> When persons manifest the least kindness and love to me, O
> what power it has over my mind, while the opposite course has a

tendency to harrow up all the harsh feelings and depress the human mind. (*Teachings of the Prophet Joseph Smith*, sel. Joseph Fielding Smith [1976], 240)

Keep these pointers in mind as you work with your companion:

1. Put obedience first. Obey the mission rules and mission president first, even if your companion does not want to. Obedience comes *before* harmony.

2. Always look to build, not to criticize. Be positive. Nobody likes hearing someone who is constantly negative. Your positive attitude will create an atmosphere where the Spirit can guide you and your companion to great success. Correction should only be given with the intent to help, and then should immediately be followed by the expression of love (see D&C 121:39–46).

3. Use companionship inventory as precious time. Discuss personal feelings about the work, and set specific goals to work better as a team. Sit next to each other, rather than across from each other in a "confrontational" position. Sincerely pray with your companion about what you really need: For yourselves, investigators, and the leaders. Set goals, by the Spirit, that are attainable (within your grasp, but not too easy), measurable, and specific: "Stretch, but don't overwhelm."

Trusting Your Mission President

Trust the Mission President enough to tell him about the obedience of yourself and your companion. Sometimes it's not easy. It's never, ever wrong, however, to keep the Mission President well informed of everything, and all the details involved. Your companion will thank you for it later. Either way, eternal faithfulness and respect are far more important than personal popularity. After all, would you rather have been just a "good buddy," or an "eternal hero?"

What can you do *before* your mission to prepare for this exact course of obedience and trust in God's chosen leaders? Look for what needs correcting in your life and decide now to change it by enlisting the help of others, and the Bishop if appropriate. Get out a piece of paper, write down things you need to improve, and start working on changing them now by setting goals. Your parents and close friends are also excellent resources.

Your Role in Converting Others

Your goal in teaching investigators should be their long-term conversion and activity in the Church. Ammon's preaching is a perfect example.

> And as sure as the Lord liveth, so sure as many as believed, or as many as were brought to the knowledge of the truth, through the preaching of Ammon and his brethren, according to the spirit of revelation and of prophecy, and the power of God working miracles in them—yea, I say unto you, as the Lord liveth, as many of the Lamanites as believed in their preaching, and were converted unto the Lord, *never did fall away*. (Alma 23:6; italics added)

That's great retention. *Retention* is when an investigator is baptized and remains active in the Church. The best retention starts with properly finding investigators, teaching investigators by the power of the Spirit, then baptizing.

Finding. How do you find people to teach? Work with the members and the Lord. Pray for it. Live for it. Don't get discouraged, and never be afraid to knock any door, talk to any person, or invite without apology anyone you find. Don't write off people as "non-investigator material" until you first share the gospel with them. One missionary asked a man in the street, without hesitation, if he would come to Church the upcoming Sunday. The man did, and was baptized soon after. Be bold. As a missionary, you are authorized to call people to repentance. It takes guts; it takes passion for the gospel; and, most of all, it takes an unwavering commitment and faith in Jesus Christ.

Teaching. How do you teach with the Spirit? The greatest answer is found in Doctrine and Covenants 50:22: "Wherefore, he that preacheth and he that receiveth, understand one another, and both are edified and rejoice together."

Some missionaries teach hundreds of discussions without any concern for the understanding or feelings of investigators, and the results show—they are not invited back to teach a second time. Can you know if your investigators are feeling the Spirit as you are teaching them? Yes, sir (or ma'am). The way you can know is that you and he or she will (1) *understand one another*, (2) *be edified*, and (3) *rejoice together*. What a powerful lesson, yet so fundamental.

Make no mistake about it: Great teaching requires serious effort. It requires the *participation* of the people you are teaching. People don't invite you in their homes so that you can lecture them. They invite you in so they can be changed by the power of the Holy Ghost. The way to guide others to change their lives is through active participation. Think of Jesus Christ and Peter. Why did the Savior ask Peter if he loved Him all those times? (see John 21:15–17) He was helping Peter to internalize the doctrine, to *own* it—to make it his.

Powerful teaching requires adapting the message to the capacity of the people you are teaching. Their background, understanding, and education will be different than any other person you have ever taught (that's part of the adventure!). So why should the message be the same?

Imagine for a moment you are sent on vacation to a faraway island to enjoy coconuts and the company of friendly monkeys. Since you are far away from your family, and you have so many people to write (and so little time to do so, since you are enjoying the sun, beach, coconuts, and companionship of jovial monkeys), you decide to simply write one letter and then photocopy it and send it to everybody, each week. The letter says, "I'm doing well. The coconuts are great, and the monkeys are happy." If you sent that same letter to every person in your family every week, how would they start to feel? What would they think about how you are *really* doing? They would have no idea, and they would probably become very frustrated. That is how investigators feel when we don't adapt our message to meet their needs. And investigator frustration leads to missionary rejection.

Adapting the message means sharing the message with feelings, experiences, examples, compliments, questions, scriptures, and testimony that fit the audience. You can learn to do this right now by simply doing it in whatever calling you have or with friends or family. The next time you want to share a precious gospel truth with someone, ask yourself first, "How can I get this person to *want* to apply this principle in their life?" Approach every situation this way, and you will discover powerful change occurring all around you.

The overall vision of your teaching as a missionary is *not* that one day, when you leave the area, the people say to you, "Elder/Sister, you've helped us so much, we don't know what we'll ever do without you!" If they say that to you, you have failed in a serious way. They ought to instead say to you, "I have my Book of Mormon, and my revelation from God through prayer. Elder/Sister thank you for your help, but because of you I don't need you anymore! Bye! (Have a great life!)" Can you feel the difference?

Baptism. On this path to real retention, do not forget the unquestionable power of the fundamentals of faith, repentance, and baptism. While preparing people for baptism, begin with the end in mind. What's your mission? It is not to simply fill time slots in your weekly calendar. You are to instill faith in the Lord Jesus Christ in the people. This will lead them to repentance and major changes in their lives that come from being baptized into the Lord's Church and receiving the gift of the Holy Ghost. Ultimately, it will lead them to the temple.

Sometimes, missionaries worry if it is their business preaching repentance or finding out about peoples' lives with the intent to help them change. *You are in the business of saving souls.* There is no excuse not to help people along their path to conversion. After all, people respect frankness, boldness, and invitations to repent when they are shared in the spirit of meekness and love. Set aside any pride or fear that might keep you from boldly challenging others to live the gospel.

True conversion leads right into the waters of baptism. Do all you can to help people prepare for this important step. The Lord expects that converts to His Church fulfill specific criteria before baptism. If the people aren't prepared, they can't be baptized at that moment. It's that simple. This is crucial, because you will be actively preparing people to take this major step through the door to eternal life, even baptism. What are the Lord's specific criteria?

And again, by way of commandment to the church concerning the manner of baptism—All those who humble themselves before God and desire to be baptized, and come forth with broken hearts and contrite spirits, and witness before the church that they have truly repented of all their sins, and are willing to take upon them the name of Jesus Christ, having a determination to serve him to the end, and truly manifest by their works that they have received of the Spirit of Christ unto the remission of their sins, shall be received by baptism into his church. (D&C 20:37)

Memorize this scripture. It is the essence of baptismal preparation. To be baptized, people must be completely repentant. They must believe in God, Jesus Christ, Joseph Smith, the current prophet, and the Church. They must feel worthy. They must be willing to live the law of chastity (not participating in any sexual relationship outside of marriage), the law of tithing, the Word of Wisdom, and the Sabbath day (including partaking of the sacrament weekly and serving fellow members). They must be fully committed to covenant with God to take upon themselves the name of Christ, keep His commandments throughout their life, and strive to be faithful.

What can you do to prepare people to achieve these lofty goals? First (and unquestionably most important), live them yourself. Second, teach the people in a way that constantly inspires them to commit and do these things. You are training a covenant people. You are preparing them to be clean before the Lord. This is the greatest work on the planet. It is an awesome responsibility. By taking it seriously, you qualify yourself for the companionship of the Lord and His Spirit in this daunting task.

Once people are baptized, continue blessing them through your testimony and teaching. Help them stay active by working with members and leaders to bless the new converts. It will be hard. Satan hates great teaching, conversion, baptism, and retention. When you decide to be a powerful missionary for the Lord, you voluntarily put a giant target on your head. Satan will be fighting you twenty-four hours a day, without breaks. Shouldn't you and I be just as committed, but to the truth? Such hard work will pay off. Retention of new members is the most wonderful thing in the world. And you're going to make it happen.

Awesome Activation. Less-active individuals will become active in the Church by having a friend, a responsibility, and the good word. It's always best "to love people into the Church." Help them in their responsibility, first by helping them to fulfill all the commitments they have made in the discussions, like reading the scriptures, praying, keeping the Sabbath day holy, obeying the law of chastity and Word of Wisdom, and fulfilling the threefold mission of the Church. Help people keep their commitments, and you truly prepare them for eternity.

On my mission, we taught the Campos and Diaz families. Each had particular challenges, but my companion and I knew what both families needed most was friends in the Church who could inspire them into full Church activity. We worked with the bishop to find "missionary families" who went to work to help the Campos and Diaz families to feel part of that great, big ward family. After their baptisms, each received a calling. Felipe Campos soon became first counselor in his ward and Rosa Diaz became second counselor in the Relief Society. They were fed the good word by stake missionaries who taught them new member discussions.

New members are like little children in the gospel. Don't ever fall into the trap of thinking, "They're baptized now, they don't need us anymore." Too many missionaries find, with such an attitude, new converts walk out the back door of the Church, never to come back.

As you activate people into the Church, like Alma did in times of old, you may find sad situations. One of the saddest things is to see someone who has given up. With an "eye of faith," you can tactfully attack such situations with hope and assurance that Heavenly Father can save that person. A companionship in my mission taught a family who were the pioneers of the area but who had been inactive for over fifteen years. Under the direction of the bishop, they worked hard to teach that family the doctrine they had forgotten. The missionaries taught them about baptism, and about Jesus Christ's power to strengthen us in adversity. When that family walked back into Church, it was truly a miracle. All eyes were fixed on them, as a warm gratitude filled the entire chapel. Such miracles happen only when missionaries go through the proper channels of authority, and work with the Spirit.

Handling Difficult Questions

One worry missionaries often face is how they will be able to answer all the difficult questions or overcome fear and anxiety about sharing the gospel. Know that some people, especially some pastors from other churches, may be out to get you. They may want to "Bible Bash," or create contention to argue their point. Take comfort in the scripture that promises, "If ye are prepared ye shall not fear" (D&C 38:30). Note that it doesn't say, "If ye are prepared ye shall be able to answer all their questions." Tell them, "I don't know" when you don't. People respect honesty more than wrong answers.

The Lord forewarned His servants in Doctrine and Covenants 43:15, "Again, I say, hearken ye elders [and sisters] of my church, whom I have appointed: Ye are not sent forth to be taught, but to teach the children of men the things which I have put into your hands by the power of my Spirit." You may come in contact with doctors, lawyers, CEOs or political leaders but *you* will have been called and authorized to teach *them* by the power of the Spirit of God.

People may hit you with seemingly difficult questions. In such situations, remember the wise counsel of Alma:

> It is given unto many to know the mysteries of God; nevertheless they are laid under a strict commandment that they shall not impart only according to the portion of his word which he doth grant unto the children of men, according to the heed and diligence which they give unto him. (Alma 12:9)

Do not make a habit of discussing topics that an unprepared heart will not understand. For an investigator who does not understand basic faith or repentance to ask about the specific purposes of polygamy in Church history is like a four-year-old who doesn't know basic arithmetic to ask, "What is calculus?" Teach people from their level, helping them understand the basics *first*.

What can you do in situations where difficult questions about the doctrine come up? Follow the Spirit (I know, it *sounds* so easy). There is something about a consistent, piercing conviction and testimony that cause it to ring in the heart for a long time. Think of the rock-hard-hearted lawyer Zeezrom, whose battle against the Lord's anointed almost cost Alma and Amulek their lives (see Alma 12–15). Remember how the testimony of those powerful missionaries shattered his disbelief, transformed his heart, and ultimately made him missionary material. With the Spirit, you can have the same effect.

You may feel nervous, awkward, scared, or anxious about sharing the gospel. As far as I know, they haven't created a "fearless missionary pill" yet (if you find them somewhere, give me a call). Your key is to share the gospel with power, despite your weakness. Yes, you may mess up sometimes. That's okay. Congratulations! That means you're human. You may be afraid the message of the Restored Gospel will *shock* the people. That's the point! They've likely never heard this message before, and they need to *feel it*. It's going to wake them up, and it has to, if it's going to have the effect it needs to in their lives.

Whenever prompted to teach someone a certain way, do it. This course of complete obedience to the Spirit of the Lord as you teach will not be easy. It never was. It will be both difficult and thrilling—difficult, because it requires the very best of you in situations you will have never encountered before; thrilling because anything can happen in this, the greatest adventure of all—coming unto Jesus Christ.

TEACH BY THE POWER OF THE SPIRIT

The following is a worksheet to empower you to teach with greater power and the Spirit. These principles have helped missionaries for thousands of years to teach like God. Apply them now and watch how you become an instrument in the Lord's hands. As you teach, be flexible to the promptings of the Spirit (note: robots do not make good missionaries). Measure yourself and your teaching against the criteria provided. Look for and create opportunities to teach, by sharing scriptures, testimony, and spiritual experiences with friends and family and then rate your performance to become better.

Love Others: Love is the great motivator (see Moro. 7:45).

Elder/Sister Scrub	Elder/Sister Average	Elder/Sister Powerful
• *Rude, judgmental, argumentative, or apathetic*	• *Considerate, candid, and caring*	• *Loving and completely focused on the needs and salvation of others*
• *Does not manifest love or care for others*	• *Manifests some love for others*	• *Shows concern, love, and Christlike charity to people*

Serve Others: Service changes people (see Mosiah 2:17).

Elder/Sister Scrub	Elder/Sister Average	Elder/Sister Powerful
• *Does not serve or seek to understand others*	• *Tries to serve and understand others but does not do enough*	• *Focuses with complete sincerity on others and helps them with their particular needs*

Proclaim the Truth: The truth will set you free (see John 8:32).

Elder/Sister Scrub	Elder/Sister Average	Elder/Sister Powerful
• *Teaches incorrect or inappropriate doctrine*	• *Proclaims powerful truths, but digresses or avoids key doctrines*	• *Teaches basic and correct doctrine with humility and faith*
• *Doesn't help others "liken" the truth to themselves*	• *Tries to help others "liken" truth*	• *Helps others apply truths with the help of the Spirit*

Seek the Spirit: The Spirit is the real teacher (see John 14:26).

Elder/Sister Scrub	Elder/Sister Average	Elder/Sister Powerful
• *No influence of the Holy Ghost*	• *Some influence of the Spirit present*	• *Powerful influence of the Spirit*
• *Teaching is mechanical, static, and not conducive to the Spirit*	• *Seeks Spirit through using a variety of means (testimony, experiences, scriptures, etc.)*	• *Seeks Spirit through heart- felt teaching, personalized to receiver*

Help Others to Make and Keep Commitments:
Inspire them to become covenant keepers (see Alma 39:16).

Elder/Sister Scrub	Elder/Sister Average	Elder/Sister Powerful
• *Invites others to live the gospel in a weak or otherwise unclear way*	• *Offers specific invitations*	• *Inspires with powerful, motivating invitations to live the gospel*
• *Coerces or pressures people to make commit- ments*	• *Does not infringe on agency*	• *Guides others with charity along the path of righteousness*

PRODUCER'S POWER TIP

As you teach with power and boldness, you never forget that the Lord will back you up, as will His angels (not a bad team to work with).

> And whoso receiveth you, there I will be also, for I will go before your face. I will be on your right hand and on your left, and my Spirit shall be in your hearts, and mine angels round about you, to bear you up. (D&C 84:88)

WRITER'S CORNER

Think of someone who needs the gospel in his or her life—a less-active member or a friend from another faith. Who is it and what can you do to effectively share the gospel with him or her?

_____

_____

_____

_____

_____

_____

_____

_____

DIRECTOR'S ACTION

Pray for that person to soften his or her heart to the gospel and show love to him or her. Invite him or her to church activities, to listen to the missionaries, or to accept a copy of the Book of Mormon with your testimony written in it. Hopefully that person will accept your invitation! If he or she does not at this time, be patient and keep praying for him or her (most people who join the Church do so after about seven contacts with members of the Church!). Your diligent gospel-sharing efforts are never in vain, and—in the final analysis—it will be as though that person accepted it. Remember that the Lord will prepare the way.

CHAPTER TWELVE

Preparation "In All Things"

Life in the mission is not all roses. In fact, it can be extremely hard. You will probably not be baptizing every day. There may even be times when, in the midst of the sweat, blood, and tears, you feel like you want to give in. Your mission will require you to do things you have never done or perhaps imagined before, and stretch you to the very threshold of spiritual progress. The question is, then, what can you do NOW to prepare for it all?

To adapt what C. S. Lewis said:

> The [missionary] way is different: harder, and easier. Christ says "Give me All. I don't want so much of your time and so much of your money and so much of your work: I want You. I have not come to torment your natural self, but to kill it. No half-measures are any good. I don't want to cut off a branch here and a branch there, I want to have the whole tree down. I don't want to drill the tooth, or crown it, or stop it, but to have it out. Hand over the whole natural self, all the desires which you think innocent as well as the ones you think wicked—the whole outfit. I will give you a new self instead. In fact, I will give you Myself: my own will shall become yours." (*Mere Christianity* [New York: Touchstone, 1980], 169)

Elder Jeffrey R. Holland wrote:

> Anyone who does any kind of missionary work will have occasion to ask, Why is this so hard? . . . Why can't our success be more

rapid? Why aren't there more people joining the Church? . . . Why isn't the only risk in missionary work that of pneumonia from being soaking wet all day and all night in the baptismal font?

. . . I have thought about this a great deal. I offer this as my personal feeling. I am convinced that missionary work is not easy because *salvation is not a cheap experience.* Salvation *never* was easy. We are The Church of Jesus Christ, this is the truth, and He is our Great Eternal Head. How could we believe it would be easy for us when it was never, ever easy for Him? It seems to me that missionaries and mission leaders have to spend at least a few moments in Gethsemane. Missionaries and mission leaders have to take at least a step or two toward the summit of Calvary.

Now, please don't misunderstand. I'm not talking about anything anywhere near what Christ experienced. That would be presumptuous and sacrilegious. But I believe that missionaries and investigators, to come to the truth, to come to salvation, to know something of this price that has been paid, will have to pay a token of that same price.

For that reason I don't believe missionary work has ever been easy, nor that conversion is, nor that retention is, nor that continued faithfulness is. I believe it is supposed to require some effort, something from the depths of our soul. (*Ensign*, Mar. 2001, 15)

As you strive to be the very best you can, you will surely encounter challenges along the way, but the key is how you deal with them. If you want, deep down, to have a successful mission, no one will be able to keep that from happening.

Volumes of books could be written about the blessings of missionary service with the Lord. The Lord hinted at this when He declared:

And if it so be that you should labor all your days in crying repentance unto this people, and bring, save it be one soul unto me, how great shall be your joy with him in the kingdom of my Father!

And now, if your joy will be great with one soul that you have brought unto me into the kingdom of my Father, how great will be your joy if you should bring many souls unto me! (D&C 18:15–16)

Love: The Greatest Motivation

Sharing the gospel is not always an easy task, but it becomes easier if we have faith and a motivating love for others. The Savior said:

Thou shalt love the Lord thy God with all thy heart, and with all thy soul, and with all thy mind. This is the first and great commandment. And the second is like unto it, Thou shalt love thy neighbor as thyself. On these two commandments hang all the law and the prophets. (Matt. 22:37–40)

You are to love God above all else. How can you love someone if you don't know him? So, first, get to know your Heavenly Father. Faith is a product of trust, and comes from loving God; a belief that Jesus Christ suffered and died for each of us and is glorified and lives today with Father.

You must love others as yourself, so you must first have hope in yourself. Hope is confidence that you, like Christ, will resurrect and live again with Heavenly Father. Mormon, speaking of hope, said, in Ether 12:32: "wherefore man must hope, or he cannot receive an inheritance in the place which thou hast prepared." Hope comes through faithfully living the commandments.

Once you have obtained hope, you can truly love others. This is charity. The primary answer to "What is charity?" is "the pure love of Christ." There is nothing more powerful, or more motivating to men and women to feel love and trust. There is nothing like charity that will change those around you, and motivate them to return to Heavenly Father.

No Regrets

Live your mission with no regrets! How can you serve a mission with no regrets? First of all, what is a *regret*? It is a sense of sorrow or guilt for having done or not having done something. If you give your best, you will have no reason to regret. Your journey to become better through service to others will be understood as necessary, but you will not regret. Remember also, that your best today will not be sufficient tomorrow.

One powerful sister missionary declares: "Be Obedient! Don't keep one foot in the world and one foot in the mission. Missionaries who do that never have the spiritual experiences they want out here, because they are not fully dedicating themselves to the Lord."

Through obedience, you are blessed spiritually and temporally (see Mosiah 2:41). It is interesting that, in the long run, we ultimately will get what we want. If we want a faithful eternal companion and if we want to be in the Celestial Kingdom, we will be there. Our works follow our true desires like a toddler follows his mom. We can only gain what we truly believe and expect of ourselves.

But, what if no one's watching? "No one will ever see me disobey that small rule," some missionaries say, trying to justify their actions. Heavenly Father can see your every move. Of this there is no doubt. On the eternal camera of life, every move, word, and thought is recorded. The truth on the mission, as in life, is this: If you obey, you will be blessed; if you don't, you won't. Lehi, who understood this concept of obedience to Heavenly Father's commandments, said to his sons:

> Inasmuch as ye shall keep [the Lord's] commandments ye shall prosper in the land; but inasmuch as ye will not keep [His] commandments ye shall be cut off from [His] presence. (2 Ne. 1:20)

One day, you will look back on your mission and preparation time before your mission, and say to yourself, "I did my very best to serve the Lord for that time! Even though I could have slacked off, I *didn't*. Even though it was hard, I worked harder. I have *no regrets* because I used the Lord's time the very best I knew how." Your life will be blessed forever for that service.

Expecting More

Elder Neal A. Maxwell declared the power of high expectations:

> Our task is avoiding unnecessary mediocrity, too, and our toler-
> ance of poor performance by ourselves and others is, at times,
> not tolerance at all, but lazy leadership. By setting Church stan-
> dards clearly and helping ourselves and others to grow within
> these standards in mind-stretching and ability-stretching ways we
> will experience infinite variety in outcome, but for the indi-
> vidual, this can result in closing the gap between what he [or she]
> is and what he [or she] might become. (*A More Excellent Way*
> [1967], 34)

It is always more difficult to raise the expectation, but isn't that
what the gospel is all about? How are we ever to become gods, if we
don't act like Heavenly Father?

You have got to *want* to help others. It has to be deeply embedded
in your entire system. The sons of Mosiah were such powerful
teachers because they had such a powerful desire.

> Now they were desirous that salvation should be declared to
> every creature, for they could not bear that any human soul
> should perish; yea, even the very thought that any soul should
> endure endless torment did cause them to quake and *tremble*.
> (Mosiah 28:3; italics added)

It is interesting to see how that scripture, describing how the sons
of Mosiah trembled relates to the following scriptural account of the
Lord describing His own Atonement for us:

> Which suffering caused myself, even God, the greatest of all, *to
> tremble* because of pain, and to bleed at every pore, and to suffer
> both body and spirit—and would that I might not drink the
> bitter cup and shrink. (D&C 19:18; italics added)

To truly serve others, get out of your comfort zone.
Service is a blessing, not a burden.

Never Give Up

"And Jesus said unto him, No man, having put his hand to the plough, and looking back, is fit for the kingdom of God." (Luke 9:62) This scripture means a great deal to me because of a particular mission experience.

One night, my companion and I arrived home at 9:30 P.M. from a hard day's work, happy with the efforts we had made. The phone rang. I picked it up, and my mission president's voice cracked as he said, "Elder Deaver, your father just had a stroke. He's in critical condition, and will probably die tonight."

The next thing I knew, I was sitting in front of my desk, where I had worked, studied, and sweat for one and a half years; in a place where I felt I had literally given my soul to the Lord and the people. I was in shock. I simply could not believe it, and I couldn't be easily comforted. These things were always supposed to happen to *other* people. How could it be me? Fortunately, my companion was a spiritual giant. We knelt down and began to fast for understanding; we wanted to understand the will of the Lord—still, in my heart, I was pained, and suffering. I didn't sleep that whole night.

We went out to preach that morning with a desire to find some listening soul. My companion, an Idaho cowboy, who made about three steps to my one, led the way. We arrived at the home of the Reyes family. A woman invited us in, and we sat down at the table of the dining room and started a discussion. She was confused about the purpose of life. She had seen family members die and didn't understand why. In my heart, I somehow knew that this opportunity would arise, though I still had an emotional hole in me, where it felt like my dad was missing. Even though I felt weak, I knew it was time for me to bear testimony. I had testified about the eternal nature of families during my whole mission, but did I really know *now*?

This was my test, my time to shine. I shared my part of the discussion, and the moment came when I bore testimony that families can be together forever. The woman we were teaching was touched deeply as the Spirit testified. Families are forever. That is our message. The Book of Mormon is a book about families; the plan is to save the family of Heavenly Father.

My father passed on and I managed to not only live through the ordeal, but grow in faith and feeling in the gospel. I came to know Jesus Christ like I never had before, and I even felt the presence of my father with me in the mission field. As you become a full-time representative of the Lord, set aside all of your worldly concerns, and focus strictly on the work. As a result, you will find power in the Lord Jesus Christ, who strengthens you.

Facing and Overcoming Challenges

You will face challenges of completely different shapes and sizes. Remember the stripling warriors, with their two thousand, compared to the innumerable army of the Lamanites? You may face investigators whose families object to them becoming members of the Church, people who harshly reject the gospel, or even active members who let go of the truth. You may feel your test is so hard that you cannot overcome it, but you will. You may feel like no one could ever understand what you're going through, but someone can. Your Savior is always there for you and always will be. Check out the words of Elder Jeffrey R. Holland from his essay "Missionary Work and the Atonement":

> If He could come forward in the night, kneel down, fall on His face, bleed from every pore, and cry, "Abba, Father (Papa), if this cup can pass, let it pass," then little wonder that salvation is not an easy thing for us. If you wonder if there isn't an easier way, you should remember you are not the first one to ask that. Someone a lot greater and a lot grander asked a long time ago if there wasn't an easier way. . . .
>
> *When you struggle, when you are rejected, when you are spit upon and cast out, you are standing with the best life this world has ever known,* the only pure and perfect life ever lived. *You have reason to stand tall and be grateful that the Living Son of the Living God knows all about your sorrows and afflictions.* The only way to salvation is through Gethsemane and on to Calvary. The only way to eternity is through Him—the Way, the Truth, and the Life. (*Ensign*, Mar. 2001, 15; italics added)

Whenever the Lord gives us a blessing, we can expect a temptation of equal and opposite strength to be presented to us. If not, we would never progress. Brigham Young explained this concept when he declared:

> I ask, is there a reason for men and women being exposed more constantly and more powerfully, to the power of the enemy, by having visions than by not having them? There is and it is simply this—God never bestows upon His people, or upon an individual, superior blessings without a severe trial to prove them, to prove that individual, or that people, to see whether they will keep their covenants with him, and keep in remembrance what He has shown them. Then the greater the vision, the greater the display of the power of the enemy. And when such individuals are off their guard they are left to themselves, as Jesus was. . . .
>
> So when individuals are blessed with visions, revelations, and great manifestations, look out, then the devil is nigh you, and you will be tempted in proportion to the vision, revelation, or manifestation you have received. Hence thousands, when they are off their guard, give way to the severe temptations which come upon them, and behold they are gone. (*Journal of Discourses*, 205–206)

Go Out and "Give 'Em Heaven"

You will *definitely* have challenges as you hold to your decision to serve a mission. The Lord promises us the hidden blessing of "opposition in *all* things" (2 Ne. 2:11; italics added). Opposition may come to you in the form of peer pressure to do the wrong things, feelings of unworthiness, or direct opposition from loved ones. Make up your mind now! Make up your mind that you will do all you can to overcome whatever opposition stands in the way of you going on a mission, and help others to do the same. If not, chances are that somebody, or something else, will make up your mind for you.

Remember: You are never alone. You have leaders and friends and family who can help you. Though you can expect difficult challenges, you can know that Jesus Christ is always there for you. He is. He is fully aware of your capabilities and your shortcomings, so He knows exactly how to best help you to reach your divine potential (see Alma 7:12). He sees you as you really are, that is, what you have the potential to become. So, next time you feel that Satan is trying to mess things up for you, remember that you are a child of God, with divine potential.

My hope is that this book helps you in your service to the Lord. There is no work greater than this, no time more important than now; and there's no excuse for mediocrity. Jesus Christ lives and loves you. This is His work. Joseph Smith saw Him and Heavenly Father, and brought forth the Book of Mormon. A prophet today speaks with Jesus Christ. Adventures in teaching await you. They are modern miracles. No one can do what you need to do exactly as well as you. This is your time, and the adventure awaits . . .

PRODUCER'S POWER TIP

"Therefore, O ye that embark in the service of God, see that ye serve him with all your heart, might, mind and strength, that ye may stand blameless before God at the last day" (D&C 4:2).

DIRECTOR'S ACTION

Review your mission story, rethink your commitment to your goals you have set for yourself, and now make it happen.

APPENDIX

Answers to Big Questions

What's the first day at the Missionary Training Center (MTC) like?

Your first day in the MTC you will go to a large meeting where you will hear about . . . missionary work (surprise!). After the meeting has ended, you will be asked to exit one way, as your family exits out the other. It can be a sad, but joyous moment, as tears are often shed. Even "tough guys" cry at these things (so, get your Kleenex ready). Next, you will move on to a series of orientation meetings, and your MTC training will have begun.

How long will I be in the MTC?

If you are going stateside, you will probably be trained for three weeks. If you go to a foreign country, it will be longer, probably between two and four months.

What will I do at the MTC?

Your training will include gospel study, teaching with power, and studying a new language—if applicable. You will hear General Authorities speak. In addition, you will have a branch president, who will interview and give you counsel—like your mission president in the field you labor.

Your MTC district will consist of anywhere between two and twelve missionaries; it could have elders and sisters, or just elders. Create unity in your district by getting to know and serving each person. You will likely have three different teachers in the MTC—one in the morning, one in the afternoon, and one at night. They will assist you in learning doctrine, understanding the gospel, and perhaps speaking a language. Treat them nicely (please?).

Take advantage of every precious minute in the Missionary Training Center. There is no worldly music or distractions. Everything is focused on the work, as should you be. For some missionaries who don't like the idea of rules and structure, the MTC is "spirit prison." For missionaries who understand the importance of their call, the MTC is a "piece of heaven."

As a missionary in the MTC, you will have a schedule with specific places to be, and things to do at certain hours. Say good-bye to the word "nap"—it will no longer be part of your vocabulary! Every hour in the MTC is packed with opportunities to stretch and push to have spiritual experiences.

In the MTC, you will probably feel like the scarecrow from Wizard of Oz, with teachers opening up your head and stuffing it full of missionary skills and doctrine. You may be overwhelmed and, as a result, impatient sometimes with yourself. Stay poised and relaxed even when things get tough, while maintaining your hard working edge. It's a difficult balance, but it can be done.

What's the food like at the MTC cafeteria?

The MTC food, contrary to some opinions, is actually pretty good. You can select anything from Lucky Charms to chips, ice cream, or salad. Don't be surprised if you find, when you leave the MTC, that the food you make in the field is less desirable.

Can I play sports in the MTC?

Yes, but be careful. Too many missionaries go out and break bones by doing something stupid on (or sometimes off) the court. One missionary had to be home several months because of a sports-related injury, and lost precious mission time because of it. So, be smart. Also, when playing sports, and this applies equally in the mission field, make sure you have the proper attitude. Nothing will lose members and investigators faster than a missionary who wants to "talk trash," or play too rough. Your attitude will affect how others feel about the Church. You might feel that is something unfair or hard. It should be. Discipleship is hard, and it requires maximum self-control.

What do they mean by "quiet dignity" at the MTC?

As a missionary, you are a "Mini General Authority." There are, in fact, very few people in this world who can say that they officially represent the Church. You will be required to live a higher standard, a "Celestial standard" (see D&C 88:22). Powerful missionaries have a special attribute in their countenances—*quiet dignity* (that is, they are *not* performing death-defying wrestling techniques on one another in class).

So how would I define quiet dignity? To be quiet, in this case, does not refer to always keeping your mouth shut. Quiet dignity refers to your attitude, and that it should be, as Alma counseled his son Shiblon, "sober," or reverent. To show respect to others and ourselves shows respect to Heavenly Father. To demonstrate reverence, and appropriate humor, is to show love for the Almighty.

Where will I be called to serve?

I don't know. That's part of the adventure!

When is the best time to serve a mission?

Basically, for men, the age that the Lord designates is from nineteen to about twenty-six, but generally not older; for women, from twenty-one on.

How many Mission Presidents will I have?

You may just have one, or may end up having two during your mission. They are generally called for three years and labor full-time in the work of the Lord as well. Follow the counsel and suggestions of your current bishop to be powerfully prepared to do the same with your mission president.

What are District Leaders, Zone Leaders, and Assistants to the President?

Each is a calling given to some elders by the mission president as an added responsibility, though you are not set apart again to be one. A district is composed of anywhere from four to eight missionaries, and a zone of eight to twenty missionaries. Do yourself a favor and don't aspire to leadership positions. You will probably be given added responsibility if and when you are able to handle the responsibilities you already have, but that's what it is—a responsibility.

Leadership is not at all bad, but a quest solely for personal glory is. You don't have to be assistant to the mission president (AP) during your mission to be a success. In Doctrine and Covenants 121:36–46, you'll find a powerful summary of eternal leadership principles that will help you govern and serve in Godlike fashion.

How will I ever learn a new language if I have never studied it before?

The Lord knows the language perfectly, and He will help you if you work hard to develop the gift of tongues. It is real. One evangelist man on my mission asked us if we had ever spoken in tongues, as if it were some once-in-a-lifetime experience, and we said, "Yes, every day." (He was very surprised.)

How will I know what to bring into the field?

With your calling, you will receive specific instructions about things to bring to the field. Follow those instructions with exactness to get off on a good foot.

What will the people be like where I serve?

Good question. Encyclopedias and the Internet are great sources to investigate the people, the culture, and food of your future destination. Do your homework about the people and it will add a strong dimension to your mission. It is also beneficial to study, beforehand, whatever language you will be speaking.

Some missionaries find people extremely prepared for conversion, whereas others find it a great challenge to discover even one listening ear. Keep an open mind. Remember that the Lord knows what He is doing when he calls you, and that He doesn't make mistakes. Wherever you are assigned, you will do a great amount of good.

What are my best tools in this spiritual war?

Number one is your testimony. A close second, in regard to missionary work, is the Book of Mormon (see Book of Mormon title page). Another powerful tool in your spiritual war is prayer. Prayer changes hearts, especially your own. Prayer brings the powers of heaven right into the living room of the family you teach. When investigators have serious questions, ask them to kneel down with you—during the discussion—and ask God for the answer. When the investigator exercises true faith, you will find plenty of spiritual solutions.

Is it true there are missionaries who go home early?

Unfortunately, yes. They are, however, few and far between. Missionaries who prepare themselves thoroughly and daily find themselves happily engaged in the work of the Lord, with no desire whatsoever to leave (in fact, great missionaries couldn't be convinced to go home).

How many missionaries are there in the world?

There are approximately 60,000 missionaries in the world today, though that number fluctuates. That makes the ratio of missionaries to people in the world about one missionary to every 110,000 people. That's what the Lord means when He says "chosen." Do you like the odds? The Lord expects a lot out of you, just like He did with the stripling warriors.

Now, you will be part of *the* most important work that you will ever and can ever be involved in—the work of saving souls. Nothing compares to it. No college degree can equal it. No multimillion-dollar professional football contract even comes close to it. No presidential election even scratches the surface of what you are to be involved in.

How often will I read the scriptures in the mission field?

Every day. Search your scriptures for thirty minutes each day (but not on your bed, where you'll fall asleep). Mark scriptures that impact and impress you. Search both chronologically (reading from start to finish) and by topic, using the Topical Guide.

What is the hardest thing for a missionary to do?

This is a great question, and it has as many answers as there are returned missionaries. One of the hardest things for missionaries to bear is when a family progresses toward baptism and suddenly stops listening to the message. It is devastating. And, for all intents and purposes, it should be. It is devastating for Heavenly Father.

It should be equally devastating to you when investigators don't fulfill their commitments, and you need to help them feel that. All the great missionaries have experienced it; Alma, Nephi, Lehi, and Helaman all did. When your investigators have not fulfilled what you have invited them to do, you ought to be devastated. Why? Because if the commitments you offer to the investigators (reading the Book of Mormon, praying to know if it is true, being baptized, and so on) are not important to you, there is no way that they will ever be important to the people you teach. The best, and *only real*, teachers are those who have already treaded the path, and are patiently, but persistently guiding truth-seekers through footsteps they have already tread.

Another headache is difficult companions. You may, at times, with a certain companion, wonder how he or she ever got a body. And though they may deserve a swift kick in the britches, that's never a solution. You will find, hopefully, that such companions can be an opportunity for you to grow. Your job may be to handle even the most rebellious of rebels and strengthen them in the Spirit. After all, you might eventually have children who are like your most difficult companion was.

What other reading do you suggest for better mission preparation?

Read any talks and quotes from General Authorities on missionary work, as well as your scriptures, particularly the experiences of the sons of Mosiah in the Book of Mormon (see Alma 17–19). Look for principles you can apply right now. Search the Doctrine and Covenants and the New Testament, mainly the teachings of Jesus Christ—powerful mission manuals.

How do you feel about your mission?

It has absolutely changed my life. There is NOTHING more important (to that point in my life) than what I did for those two years. It brought me closer to Jesus Christ. It gave me a spiritual heart transplant, to feel love for others like Heavenly Father feels for them.

Not a day goes by that I don't remember some lesson learned in my mission; principles like humility, patience, diligence, charity, teamwork, focus—you can't buy them, and you won't find them serving yourself for two years. Your mission story, you will find, like the sons of Mosiah, will bring greater joy than you could have ever imagined (see Alma 26).

About the Author

Christopher Deaver loves teaching. A native of southern California, he served a mission in Trujillo, Peru, and later taught missionaries at the Missionary Training Center and youth at seminaries, firesides, and EFY in California, Texas, and Utah. He has a degree in art from Brigham Young University and enjoys writing, drawing, and telling dog stories from the mission. He can be contacted at knowbeforeyougo@hotmail.com.

EXCERPT FROM RAISING THE BAR
BY ED J. PINEGAR

President Hinckley recently said, "The time has come when we must raise the standards of those who are called to serve as ambassadors of the Lord Jesus Christ to the world" ("Missionary Service," *First Worldwide Leadership Training Meeting*, Jan. 2003, 17).

In today's world, the Lord needs the greatest missionaries that have ever served. They must be worthy and prepared. The Lord needs more virtuous, righteous, free-from-sin disciples—worthy in every way. He needs missionaries who are more faithful, obedient, honest, hard-working and doing the will of the Lord. He needs more doctrinally sound and testimony-bearing missionaries who are full of faith, hope, and charity; missionaries who have lived faith unto repentance; missionaries who preach the word of God by the Spirit, that people may come unto Christ; missionaries with the attributes and skills necessary to serve with all their heart, might, mind, and strength.

Elder Ballard, in his magnificent sermon in general conference entitled "The Greatest Generation of Missionaries," said:

> What we need now is the greatest generation of missionaries in the history of the Church. We need worthy, qualified, spiritually energized missionaries who, like Helaman's 2,000 stripling warriors, are "exceedingly valiant for courage and also for strength and activity" and who are "true at all times in whatsoever thing they [are] entrusted" (Alma 53:20).
>
> As an Apostle of the Lord Jesus Christ, I call upon you to begin right now—tonight—to be fully and completely worthy. Resolve and commit to yourselves and to God that from this moment forward you will strive diligently to keep your hearts, hands, and

minds pure and unsullied from any kind of moral transgression. Resolve to avoid pornography as you would avoid the most insidious disease, for that is precisely what it is. Resolve to completely abstain from tobacco, alcohol, and illegal drugs. Resolve to be honest. Resolve to be good citizens and to abide by the laws of the land in which you live. Resolve that from this night forward you will never defile your body or use language that is vulgar and unbecoming to a bearer of the priesthood.

And that is not all we expect of you, my young brethren. We expect you to have an understanding and a solid testimony of the restored gospel of Jesus Christ. We expect you to work hard. We expect you to be covenant makers and covenant keepers. We expect you to be missionaries to match our glorious message.

Now these are high standards. We understand that, but we do not apologize for them. They reflect the Lord's standards for you to receive the Melchizedek Priesthood, to enter the temple, to serve as missionaries, and to be righteous husbands and fathers. There's nothing new in them, nothing you haven't heard before. But tonight we call upon you, our young brethren of the Aaronic priesthood, to rise up, to measure up, and to be fully prepared to serve the Lord.

(*Ensign*, Nov. 2002, 47.)

We can see that the requirements have been raised. We must rise to this expectation. When we understand and appreciate doctrines, principles, concepts, and covenants of the gospel, our attitudes and behavior will change. We will be the kind of missionary the Lord expects us to be.

THE BAR HAS BEEN RAISED

President Hinckley has said, "We simply cannot permit those who have not qualified themselves as to worthiness to go into the world to speak the glad tidings of the gospel" (*First Worldwide Leadership Training Meeting*, Jan. 2003, 17).

We now understand from the First Presidency's statement on missionary work that there are transgressions that will disqualify young men and women from missionary service (see "Statement on Missionary Work from the First Presidency and the Quorum of the Twelve Apostles," 11 Dec. 2002). The Lord indeed expects us to qualify in order to serve. It is a privilege, not a right.

Worthiness and Preparedness

Elder Ballard taught us that if we are not on track, if we are not doing what is right, we must put ourselves on track. We must put ourselves in a situation where we can become worthy. He said:

> Many of you are already on this track, and we commend you for your worthiness and determination. For those of you who are not, let tonight be the beginning of your preparation process. If you find yourself wanting in worthiness, resolve to make the appropriate changes—beginning right now. If you think you need to talk to your father and your bishop about any sins you may have committed, don't wait; do it now. They will help you to repent and change so you can take your place as a member of the greatest generation of missionaries.
>
> ("The Greatest Generation of Missionaries" *Ensign*, Nov. 2002, 47–48.)

Don't wait to repent. Be prepared. We must reiterate that the bar has been raised. We cannot knowingly do wrong and then say, "Oh, I'll repent before my mission and then go." Elder Ballard emphasized this point in October 2002:

> Please understand this: the bar that is the standard for missionary service is being raised. The day of the "repent and go" missionary is over. You know what I'm talking about, don't you, my young brothers? Some young men have the mistaken idea that they can be involved in sinful behavior and then repent when they're [almost 19] so they can go on their mission at 19. While it is true that you can repent of sins, you may or you may not qualify to serve. It is far better to keep yourselves clean and pure and valiant . . .
>
> ("The Greatest Generation of Missionaries," *Ensign*, Nov. 2002, 48.)

Elders and sisters, there are consequences for sin. Sometimes, we think that when we repent, it's a single moment, an event. It is not an event. Repentance is a process. If you were to fall off a cliff, break your leg, and get a compound fracture, and then say, "Oh, I wish I hadn't done that," your leg wouldn't be healed instantly. It requires a process. It takes time. Certain things have to be done for that bone to heal. The same principle applies in preparing for a mission. Sometimes people think that if they confess and say they won't do it again, that the consequences of sin are over. They are not over. The spirit, heart, and mind often take time to heal from the consequences of sin. Let me reiterate—it is not an event. It is a process, and it will take time.

Because we don't always recognize that there are consequences of sin, many people mistakenly think they can go on a mission, no matter what they've done, if they just confess. Some will now be withheld from service because their sins are so grievous. This does not preclude them from being exalted or from being married in the temple. It merely means that at this time in their life the consequences of sin are very severe. In preparing to serve, Elder Ballard has suggested some things prospective missionaries should be doing:

- Developing a meaningful prayer relationship with your Heavenly Father.
- Keeping the Sabbath day holy.
- Working and putting part of your earnings in a savings account.
- Paying a full and honest tithing.
- Limiting the amount of time spent playing computer games. How many kills you can make in a minute with a computer game will have zero effect on your capacity to be a good missionary.
- Giving the Lord more of your time by studying the scriptures and gaining an understanding of the marvelous message of the Restoration that we have for the world.
- Serving others and sharing your testimony with them.
  ("The Greatest Generation of Missionaries," *Ensign*, Nov. 2002, 48.)

Parents, priesthood leaders, and various other friends and family should help missionaries be prepared. Brothers and sisters, seek the advice of your parents. Go to seminary. Take your missionary preparation courses at your institute or Church university. Do every needful thing. Read books on missionary work. Search the scriptures on missionary work. There are things you can do individually and things you can do as a family to help prepare. There are things you can do in your priesthood and Young Women classes, and in preparation courses held by your stake.

The most important thing is that we must prepare earlier and better. We must devote time to preparation. Being prepared as a missionary is not having a new suit or a new wardrobe or new scriptures. Being prepared as a missionary is a changing of heart, of mind, of soul. It is the very essence of becoming a disciple of Jesus Christ.

Prophets have upheld this standard from the beginning of the missionary program.

Brigham Young states the following:

> If the Elders cannot go with clean hands and pure hearts, they had better stay here. Do not go thinking, when you arrive at the Missouri River, at the Mississippi, at the Ohio, or at the Atlantic, that then you will purify yourselves; but start from here with clean hands and pure hearts, and be pure from the crown of the head to the soles of your feet; then live so every hour. Go in that manner, and in that manner labor, and return again as clean as a piece of pure white paper. This is the way to go; and if you do not do that, your hearts will ache.
>
> (*Brigham Young, Discourses of Brigham Young,*
> sel. John A. Widtsoe [Salt Lake City: Deseret Book, 1954], 323.)

President Woodruff also noted:

> All the messengers in the vineyard should be righteous and holy men and call upon the Lord in mighty prayer, in order to prevail. It is the privilege of every Elder in Israel, who is laboring in the vineyard, if he will live up to his privileges, to have dreams, visions and revelations, and the Holy Ghost as a constant companion, that he may be able thoroughly to gather out the blood of Israel and the meek of the earth, and bring them into the fold of Christ.
>
> (Wilford Woodruff, *The Discourses of Wilford Woodruff,*
> ed. G. Homer Durham [Salt Lake City: Bookcraft, 1969], 101.)

THE DEMANDS OF MISSIONARY WORK

Worthiness must be our main focus in preparation, but it is not the only factor to consider. Physical well-being can also play a prominent role in preparing for a mission. The Brethren have recently explained: "Those individuals not able to meet the physical, mental, and emotional demands of full-time missionary work are honorably excused. . . . They may be called to serve in other rewarding capacities" ("Statement on Missionary Work from the First Presidency and the Quorum of the Twelve Apostles," 11 Dec. 2002). We must be physically healthy. We must be able to endure the rigors of missionary work. It is not easy. Sometimes we are so enthused we think we can do anything, but if you had an injured leg and were asked to run the 100-yard dash, it might not be possible to win the race. You want to win, you've done as much as you can to win, but you simply can't run fast enough because of your situation.

It is the same thing in missionary work. If you have serious physical limitations and you cannot stand the rigors of full-time serivce, it is not required of you to serve a full-time mission. Mosiah 4:27 states "it is not requisite that a man should run faster than he has strength." The Lord does not expect us to do things that we cannot do. This does not mean that we are unworthy. The Lord loves us. Remember this: earth is our mission. *Everything* on this earth is a mission from the day we are born until the day we die; we are always missionaries for the Lord Jesus Christ. We are His disciples. We can help people come unto Christ by befriending our neighbors, friends, and classmates. Everyone knows someone who is not a member of our Church. Help that person come to know that Jesus is the Christ. Befriend them. Teach them. Nurture them. Invite the missionaries to see them.

Because we're not full-time proselyting missionaries does not mean that we can't be missionaries for the Lord Jesus Christ. So if physical conditions prevent you from serving, you are honorably excused, and there should be no guilt. You can even serve Church-service missions right from home. It's a joy. I'm a Church-service missionary. I get to go teach at the Senior MTC every week. It is truly a privilege! Everyone can be a missionary every day. If physical requirements prevent you from going, be of good cheer. Heavenly Father loves you. You are his son or his daughter. You can serve in whatever way you are able while you're still at home.

Some of us struggle with emotional problems—a chemical imbalance, or whatever it might be. There are certain mental stresses that can cause panic attacks or anxiousness. These emotional stresses can affect our physical bodies in very severe ways and can prevent us from serving the Lord on a full-time mission. Unless the condition is stabilized with proper medication, the Lord and the prophet have excused us from the work. Again, these challenges have no effect on our personal worthiness or desire to serve.

If we have any physical or emotional difficulties that might prevent our full-time service, do not overburden the bishop by saying, "The Lord loves me. He will make me well," or "I have enough faith that I'll be okay." If you qualify medically and your condition is stabilized and cleared through a doctor, then you can serve full-time. But don't put guilt upon yourself. Don't beat yourself up because you're not emotionally or physically able to participate in the strains of full-time missionary service. Let the Lord guide your life and trust in His wisdom for you.

Regardless of whether we serve full-time missions, service missions, or just everyday missions, one of the great needs in today's missionary effort is more and better prepared missionaries. President Spencer W. Kimball has said:

> I am asking that we start earlier and train our missionaries better in every branch and every ward in the world. . . . I am asking for missionaries who have been carefully indoctrinated and trained through the family and the organizations of the Church, and who come to the mission with a great desire. I am asking . . . that we train prospective missionaries much better, much earlier, much longer, so that each anticipates his mission with great joy.
>
> ("When the World Will Be Converted," *Ensign*, Oct. 1974, 7.)

BEING BEYOND REPROACH

One of the best things about serving as a missionary, and preparing to serve as one, is the frequent opportunity to evaluate yourself and see if you are "beyond reproach"—innocent and pure. Personal evaluations of our lives have a way of showing our positive qualities as well as some slightly negative tendencies we might have.

To continually evaluate yourself—beginning now—you start with your head and check to see if it is "on straight," as the saying goes. Is your mind programmed to keep you moving along the straight and narrow? Is your mind in control of your life, your choices, your reactions, your actions? Or are you controlled by emotions—easy to anger, easy to self-pity, easy to have hurt feelings, quick to be jealous or resentful of another's success?

Every missionary is set apart so that he or she may be enhanced by the Spirit of God, that is, be even better at this work than he or she might naturally be. Think of the words Paul the Apostle wrote to Timothy, whom he considered his dearly beloved son: "Wherefore I put thee in remembrance that thou stir up the gift of God, which is in thee by the putting on of my hands. For God hath not given us the spirit of fear; but of power, and of love, and of a sound mind" (2 Tim. 1:6–7).

Now, as part of this important self-evaluation, move to your heart. Look deep inside. What do you see? Consider the questions listed in Alma 5 in terms of your own life and feelings.

> And now behold, I ask of you, my brethren of the church, have ye spiritually been born of God? Have ye received his image in your countenances? Have ye experienced this mighty change in your hearts?

> Do ye exercise faith in the redemption of him who created you? Do you look forward with an eye of faith, and view this mortal body raised in immortality, and this corruption raised in incorruption, to stand before God to be judged according to the deeds which have been done in the mortal body?
>
> (Alma 5:14–15.)

These revealing verses are but a fraction of the insights that come to people who read Alma and match themselves against the high standards presented in that chapter.

We are happy when we are "beyond reproach." We enjoy success. We wax confident before God and feel His approbation. We think of others before ourselves and virtue garnishes our thoughts.

You can meet the challenge. You can be a pure disciple of Jesus Christ. You can be worthy, prepared, and a clean instrument in the hands of the Lord. You can make a difference in the lives of your brothers and sisters. You can help them taste of the joy that you have. You can do all that the Lord expects you to do as you turn your will over to the Lord.

CONCLUSION

The bar has been raised. We, as future missionaries, and especially full-time proselyting missionaries, have been instructed by living prophets. We should prepare to be disciples of Jesus Christ by doing every needful thing, as well as assessing our social, emotional, intellectual, and physical health—doing our best to be as healthy as possible and leaving the rest to the Lord. Above all, we must become spiritually strong.

Your spiritual strength is so essential in serving. If, within your heart, you do not have this spirit of undying commitment to the covenant that you've made with the Lord, there will be days when you will not be able to serve as well as you should, both on and off your mission. We need spiritual strength in order to be the kind of missionaries we should be. There are souls to be saved. There are souls to be strengthened. There are souls to be rescued. There are families to be activated. There is work to be done. Wherever we are, this is part of our duty, our obligation, our calling as members of the Church and kingdom of God, disciples of the Lord Jesus Christ. Surely we can all serve in the ways that the Lord will provide for us to serve, whether as full-time missionaries, Church-service missionaries, or even as members fulfilling our Church callings. We can all serve our God and our fellowmen by helping them come unto Christ and enjoy the blessings of exaltation.

We must become missionaries to match the message, disciples of Jesus Christ, not just for a full-time mission, but for life. We need to be full of faith. We need to be moved to repentance. We must have a desire to serve. We must be living worthy of a temple recommend—we must maintain the worthiness that is expected of us in order to serve.